T0344409

Quick Recursion

Recursion is the best tool for working with trees and graphs. But perhaps you've studied recursion and decided it's too complicated. You just can't think that way. That limits the kind of programming you can do.

Good news! Recursion is actually *easy*. It's just badly taught.

See, many instructors talk about *how the computer does it*. They go on and on about what happens at each level of the recursion and how each level relates to other levels. The problem is that you can't think in multiple levels. Nobody can. And you don't have to.

This book will show you how *you* can write recursive programs. Once you understand a few simple rules, you will wonder why you ever thought recursion was complicated. You'll be able to write recursive programs quickly and easily.

Well, as quick and easy as programming ever is, anyway.

Quick Recursion

David Matuszek

CRC Press

Taylor & Francis Group

Boca Raton London New York

CRC Press is an imprint of the
Taylor & Francis Group, an **informa** business

A CHAPMAN & HALL BOOK

First edition published 2023
by CRC Press
6000 Broken Sound Parkway NW, Suite 300, Boca Raton, FL 33487-2742

and by CRC Press
4 Park Square, Milton Park, Abingdon, Oxon, OX14 4RN

CRC Press is an imprint of Taylor & Francis Group, LLC

© 2023 David Matuszek

Library of Congress Cataloguing-in-Publication Data
Names: Matuszek, David L., author.
Title: Quick recursion / David Matuszek.
Description: First edition. | Boca Raton : Taylor and Francis, 2023. | Series: Quick programming | Includes bibliographical references and index.
Identifiers: LCCN 2022041466 (print) | LCCN 2022041467 (ebook) | ISBN 9781032417585 (paperback) | ISBN 9781032417592 (hardback) | ISBN 9781003359616 (ebook)
Subjects: LCSH: Recursive programming. | Recursion theory.
Classification: LCC QA76.6 .M369 2023 (print) | LCC QA76.6 (ebook) | DDC 005.13/1--dc23/eng/20221107
LC record available at https://lccn.loc.gov/2022041466
LC ebook record available at https://lccn.loc.gov/2022041467

ISBN: 978-1-032-41759-2 (hbk)
ISBN: 978-1-032-41758-5 (pbk)
ISBN: 978-1-003-35961-6 (ebk)

DOI: 10.1201/9781003359616

Typeset in Minion
by MPS Limited, Dehradun

*To all my students
past, present, and future*

Contents

Author

I 'M DAVID MATUSZEK, known to most of my students as "Dr. Dave."

I wrote my first program on punched cards in 1963, and immediately got hooked.

I taught my first computer classes in 1970, as a graduate student in Computer Science at The University of Texas in Austin. I eventually got my PhD from there, and I've been teaching ever since. Admittedly, I spent over a dozen years in industry, but even then I taught as an adjunct for Villanova university.

I finally escaped from industry and joined the Villanova faculty full time for a few years, then moved to the University of Pennsylvania, where I directed a master's program (MCIT, master's in computer and information technology) for students coming into computer science from another discipline.

Throughout my career, my main interests have been in artificial intelligence (AI) and programming languages. I've used a *lot* of programming languages.

I retired in 2017, but I can't stop teaching, so I'm writing a series of "quick start" books on programming and programming languages. I've also written two science fiction novels, *Ice Jockey* and *All True Value*, and I expect to write more. Check them out!

If you find this book useful, it would be wonderful if you would post a review. Reviews, even critical ones, help to sell books.

And hey, if you're a former student or colleague of mine, drop me a note. I'd love to hear from you!

david.matuszek@gmail.com

Preface

R ECURSION IS CONSIDERED TO BE AN "ADVANCED" TOPIC. It shouldn't be.

When my oldest daughter was in high school, she was deeply involved in a multiplayer dungeon (MUD) game. She implemented an email system for it, using a language called Forth, which uses recursion extensively.

When she went to college, she took a programming class. After a week or so she called home and asked me, "Daddy, what are loops for?" When I explained, she said, "Why not just use recursion? It's so much simpler."

I agree.

CHAPTER 1

Understanding Recursion

1.1 A NOTE ON LANGUAGES

Any programming book needs examples, and examples have to be in some language.

This book uses two well-known languages, Java and Python 3. The code is kept simple, without any language-specific "tricks," so it should be accessible even to programmers who know neither of these languages.

That said, it is impossible to avoid all language-specific features and still have working code. Python uses indentation to show nesting of statements, while Java uses braces. To remove leading blanks, Python uses strip() while Java uses trim(). Differences such as these should not greatly obscure the examples.

1.2 RECURSIVE DEFINITIONS

A *recursive definition* is a definition in which the thing being defined occurs as part of its own definition.

DOI: 10.1201/9781003359616-1   1

Sounds circular, doesn't it? Circular definitions, in computer science as elsewhere, are valueless and should be avoided. The distinction between a recursive and a circular definition lies in the use of the work "part." Any recursive definition has two parts:

1. a noncircular part, or **basis**, which is like an ordinary definition, and directly specifies some objects that fit the definition; and

2. a recursive (circular) part, which allows you to use the objects that fit the definition in determining whether new objects also fit the definition.

Some examples should clarify these ideas.

Here is an ordinary definition:

Vowel: one of the letters "a," "e," "i," "o," "u," or "y."

Clearly, there are exactly six things that fit the above definition of a vowel. Now consider the following circular definition:

Yowl: any yowl followed by a vowel.

By this definition, any yowl followed by a vowel is also a yowl; thus, if we could find one thing which is a yowl, then any things formed by adding vowels to that yowl would themselves be yowls. The problem is in finding that first yowl. Since we have no place to start, the definition is circular, and valueless.

Now consider the following definition:

Howl:

1. the letter "h," or

2. any howl followed by a vowel.

This definition is recursive. The first part is an ordinary definition, and tells us that the letter "h" is a howl; this gives us a *basis,* or place to start. The second part is the recursive part; it tells us that, since "h" is a howl, so are "ha," "he," "hi," "ho," "hu," and "hy." But since these are howls too, so also must be "haa," "hae," ..., "hyy," .... "haaeeuooeea," etc.

Note that this is a "good" definition in the sense that some things are howls, some things are not howls, and it is easy to tell from the definition which are which. The "circularity" of the second part of the definition causes no harm because the first part provides a basis.

Recursion abounds in computer science. A typical definition of "identifier" (or "variable name"), for example, is as follows.

Identifier:

1. a letter, or

2. an identifier followed by a letter, digit, or underscore.

Notice that the definitions of both "howl" and "identifier" allow arbitrarily long strings. It is possible to write recursive definitions which limit the size of the things being defined, but in general this is neither easy nor desirable. Instead, if there must be limits, they are set by some external agency. Some programming languages, for example, allow arbitrarily long identifiers, but require that two different identifiers must differ in the first k characters, where k is set by the implementation. In the same way, the maximum length of a howl might be determined by your lung capacity.

You have probably noticed that the above definitions don't *have* to be recursive; they could be made into ordinary definitions by using the phrase "any number of ...," which can be implemented with a loop. This is true—we don't need recursion. In fact, recursion is *never* absolutely necessary, merely useful.

The definitions we have considered so far have all been examples of **direct recursion**. For an example of **indirect recursion**, consider the following pair of definitions (adapted from Lisp):

S-expression: an identifier or a list.

List: a sequence consisting of

1. a left parenthesis,

2. zero or more S-expressions separated by blanks, and

3. a right parenthesis.

Thus, the following things are lists (and also S-expressions):

```
()
(ZIP ZAP ZOT)
(ONE (TWO THREE) ((FOUR)) FIVE)
(() IXOHOXI ())
```

These definitions are **mutually recursive**: each is defined in terms of the other. The basis for the S-expression is an identifier, while the basis for the list is the sequence ().

To show that these definitions "work," consider the S-expression (NOT (HARD)).

1. (NOT (HARD)) is an S-expression because it is a list.

2. (NOT (HARD)) is a list because it consists of a left parenthesis, the two S-expressions NOT and (HARD), and a right parenthesis.

3. NOT is an S-expression because it is an identifier.

4. (HARD) is an S-expression because it is a list.

5. (HARD) is a list because it consists of a left parenthesis, the S-expression HARD, and a right parenthesis.

6. HARD is an S-expression because it is an identifier.

Q.E.D.

Of course you don't have to go through this complete process every time you see an S-expression, but we were being very formal.

Now is a good time to put in a plug for the usefulness of recursion. The definition of "list" given above may seem confusing at first (if you're not used to recursive definitions), but I challenge anyone to write a reasonable definition of "list" which is equivalent to the one given above, yet does not use any form of recursion.

1.3 A SIMPLE RECURSIVE PROCEDURE

A *recursive procedure* (or function, or method, or subroutine) is a procedure that calls itself to do part of the work.

Again, the trick is in the use of the word "part." If it called itself to do *all* of the work, the result would be an **infinite recursion** (the recursive equivalent of an infinite loop). Just as a loop does some part of the work during each iteration of the loop, so must a recursive procedure do some part of the work at each level of recursion, until eventually all the work is done.

We'll start with a simple example. This will be a function to ask the user a question that requires a yes or no answer. If the user responds with a word beginning with 'y' or 'Y,' the function will return True. If the user's response begins with 'n' or 'N,' the function will return False.

In Python:

```python
def ask_yes_or_no(question):
    answer = input(question + ' ').strip().lower()
    if len(answer) > 0:
        if answer[0] == 'y':
            return True
        if answer[0] == 'n':
            return False
    print('Please answer with yes or no.')

    # Now what?
```

In Java:

```java
private static boolean askYesOrNo(String question) {
    char answer = ' ';
    System.out.print(question + " ");
    String line = scanner.nextLine();
    if (line.length() > 0) {
        answer = line.toLowerCase().charAt(0);
        if (answer == 'y') return true;
        if (answer == 'n') return false;
    }
    System.out.println("Please answer with yes or no.");
    // Now what?
}
```

Without recursion, the obvious thing to do is to embed the code in a loop and set some kind of a flag to indicate whether the user has responded correctly. If the user doesn't answer with a yes or no, then complain and go through the loop again.

Instead of doing that, what if we just called the method again, and returned whatever it returned?

In Python:

```python
def ask_yes_or_no(question):
    answer = input(question + ' ').strip().lower()
    if len(answer) > 0:
        if answer[0] == 'y':
            return True
        if answer[0] == 'n':
            return False
    print('Please answer with yes or no.')

    return ask_yes_or_no(question)
```

In Java:

```java
private static boolean askYesOrNo(String question) {
    char answer = ' ';
    System.out.print(question + " ");
    String line = scanner.nextLine();
    if (line.length() > 0) {
        answer = line.toLowerCase().charAt(0);
        if (answer == 'y') return true;
        if (answer == 'n') return false;
    }
    System.out.println("Please answer with yes or no.");

    return askYesOrNo(question);
}
```

This code could result in an infinite recursion, but that will only happen if the user never provides an acceptable response. For code that doesn't require a user response, a few simple rules (to be described) must be followed.

1.4 FACTORIAL

The usual first example of recursion is the factorial function. We will use it for the same reason everyone else does: It is simple.

The *factorial* of a positive integer n, written $n!$, is the product of all the positive integers from 1 up to and including n. Thus, we have

```
1! == 1
2! == 1 * 2 == 2
3! == 1 * 2 * 3 == 6
4! == 1 * 2 * 3 * 4 == 24
```

and so on.

Note that, for example, 4! == 1 * 2 * 3 * 4 == (1 * 2 * 3) * 4 == 3! * 4, and in general n! == (n - 1)! * n. This leads to the following recursive definition:

The *factorial* of a positive integer n is

1. 1, if n == 0 (*base case*), or

2. (n - 1)! * n, if n > 0 (*recursive part*).

This definition leads immediately to the following Python program:

```python
def factorial(n):
    "Computes the factorial of its argument."
    if n == 0:
        return 1
    else:
        return factorial(n - 1) * n
```

Or the equivalent Java program:

```
public static int factorial(int n) {
    if (n == 0) return 1;
    else return n * factorial(n - 1);
}
```

This function has a base case (when n == 0) and a recursive part (when n is positive), and it does part of the work (multiplying by n) at each level of the recursion. Thus it seems as though the function might possibly work. But if this is the first time you have seen recursion, you may not be comfortable with it.

Some authors suggest that the best way to understand a recursive function is to trace through it, keeping track of what happens at every call and every return of the function. By all means work through such a trace, if doing so helps you believe recursion can actually work. But you should *never* think of tracing through a recursive procedure as a means of understanding, such a procedure. "Tracing through" has probably kept thousands of people from ever really understanding recursion. The purpose of this book is to describe a better technique.

1.5 THE PRINCIPLE OF INFORMATION HIDING

Perhaps the single most important tool we have for controlling the complexity of programs is modularization: breaking a single complex program up into several simpler, logically independent computations. Depending on the programming language, these are called by various names: functions, methods, procedures, etc.

Whenever a program is broken into two parts, there comes into being an **interface** between them. This interface consists of the parameter list, any global or common variables they may share between them, any results returned or exceptions raised, and often more subtle ways of information transmission. If modularization is to succeed in reducing complexity, this interface must be kept as *narrow* and as *explicit* as possible.

The best way to keep the interface narrow is to ensure that each routine does just one thing, and that that thing can be easily described in an English sentence with few or no "buts" and "excepts" in it. Keeping parameter lists short and avoiding global variables can also help.

The best way to make the interface explicit is to ensure, whenever possible, that all information transmission occurs via the parameter list, not through global variables. There are those who feel global variables should be avoided entirely, but I don't take such an extreme position. It is often more convenient to have global access to arrays and other large data structures; just take special care not to modify them accidentally.

Side effects should also be avoided. The ***main effect*** of a routine is the thing it's supposed to do; ***side effects*** are the little extra things it does. Side effects are dangerous even when they're intentional. For example, if a function factorial(n) computes n!, that's its main effect; but if it also stores the result in a global variable, that's a side effect. This is bad because it happens in the factorial function, but errors that result from this side effect will show up in any code which calls factorial. Since these routines may themselves be correct, the likely result is that the programmer spends hours trying to debug the wrong routines.

We are now in a position to state the ***Principle of Information Hiding***: *Every routine should mind its own business.* No routine should meddle in the affairs of another. Or, somewhat more formally,

- A routine should use only the information provided to it, preferably via its parameter list. If it must access global data, that fact must be clearly and unambiguously specified.

- A routine should return a single result (in Python, this could be a tuple of values) and do nothing else. If it must modify global data, that fact must be clearly and un-ambiguously specified.

- A routine should be independent of its context. For ex-ample, if some routine calls a sort method,

  - that routine should neither know nor care just how the sort method operates, so long as the sorting happens,

  - *and in addition,* the sort method should neither know nor care why its calling routine wants the sorting done.

Similar rules hold for *classes* and *objects*. An object holds various kinds of data; the class of the object holds methods to manipulate that data. An object's data should be accessed and modified *only* by the methods given in its class, *never* from outside the class.

Here are three simple examples of violations of the Principle of Information Hiding. In each case, the function is supposed to return the minimum or maximum value in a non-empty list of integers. Can you spot the violations?

```
def minimum1(numbers):
    """Return the smallest number in a list."""
    numbers.sort()
    return numbers[0]

def minimum2(numbers):
    """Return the smallest number in a list."""
    global i
    min = numbers[0]
    for i in range(1, len(numbers)):
```

```
            if numbers[i] < min:
                min = numbers[i]
        return min

def maximum(numbers):
    """Return the largest number in a list."""
    max = 0
    for i in range(0, len(numbers)):
        if numbers[i] > max:
            max = numbers[i]
    return max
```

The answers are given at the end of this section.

These examples are trivial, and in real life are not likely to cause major problems. Things get worse when the rest of the program gets more interesting.

The following skeleton program controls a two-player game between the human and the computer, in which the players alternate moves. The Principle of Information Hiding has been largely respected in this example; indeed, it is impossible to deduce from the program just which game is being played.

```
def main():
    setup()
    player = choose_who_goes_first()
    game_over = False
    while not game_over:
        if player == 'human':
            move = ask_human_for_move()
            (game_over, result) = make_move(player, move)
            player = 'computer'
        else: # player == 'computer'
            move = decide_move()
            (game_over, result) = make_move(player, move)
            player = 'human'
```

```
        print("Game over!")
        print(result)

def ask_human_for_move():
        move = input('Enter your move: ')
        if legal_move(move):
            return move
        else:
            print("That's not legal. Try again.")
            return ask_human_for_move()
```

It is possible to understand this program and verify its correctness, given very simple assumptions about what the called routines do. For example, we would expect choose_who_goes_first() to somehow decide who plays first and to set its parameter to "human" or "computer" accordingly. All information relevant to the operation of the main program is fully specified in the parameter lists.

I have not shown any of the declarations. There could be a structured variable "board" which represents a playing board; if there is only one of it, and if it is used by all routines, it might be a good idea to make "board" a global variable rather than to put it in the parameter list of every routine.

Now consider an alternate version of the same program.

```
def main():
        global k
        setup()
        choose_who_goes_first()
        while not game_over:
            if player == 'human':
                ask_human_for_move()
                check_if_move_is_legal()
                k = k - 1
                make_move()
```

```
        else: # player == 'computer'
            decide_move()
            k = k + 1
            make_move()
    print("Game over!")
    print(result)
```

Due to the many violations of the Principle of Information Hiding, it is impossible to tell whether the program is correct or not, without extensive reference to the called routines.

- What routine or routines update player? Do they do it in such a way that the main program works?

- If the human's move is not legal, has player already been updated?

- How does make_move know whose move to make?

- Where is result determined?

- When does the game end? Where is this determined?

- Is k being initialized properly? Computed properly? What is it anyway, and where is it used?

It may seem at this point that we have drifted away from the topic of recursion, and perhaps we have, since the Principle of Information Hiding applies to all programs. As we shall see in a later section, however, it has a special importance for recursive programs.

Answers to questions about information hiding violations:

1. minimum1: Sorting the list is a rather drastic side effect.

2. minimum2: The function changes the global variable "i."

3. maximum: This function assumes that the list is not composed entirely of negative numbers.

The last of these (maximum) deserves a little more explanation. As a general-purpose function, it is an error to assume that the input is not a list of negative numbers. As part of a program where this never occurs, the function will work, but it assumes too much about its context. At some future date, code may be added to the program which violates this assumption. The best solution is to fix the code; next best is to modify the comment to specify "... in a list of numbers, not all of which are negative."

1.6 WHEN TO USE RECURSION

It is an easily proved fact that you never *need* recursion; any recursive program can be changed into a non-recursive one that uses a stack. (In the same way you can prove that any program could be written in absolute binary.)

The best answer to the question of when to use recursion is, simply, when you happen to find it useful. You never just set out to "use recursion," any more than you just set out to "use a loop." You program; sometimes you use a loop, sometimes you use an array, sometimes you do input/output, and sometimes you recur.

But that's not a very useful answer when you're first getting started. We'll try to be more specific.

One good rule of thumb is to use recursion when you are processing recursively defined data structures. If you try to evaluate an arithmetic expression, for example, parentheses may be used to enclose a "subexpression" which must be evaluated first, and is an expression in its own right. If you're writing code to evaluate arithmetic expressions, there are only two reasonable ways to do this: recursively, or by "simulating" recursion with an explicit stack.

Another (equivalent) rule is to handle nested structures with recursion. As an example, in many languages, any statement may be nested in an if statement, even another if statement. There is a clear use for recursion in any processor (compiler, preprocessor, interpreter, debugger, pretty printer) for such a language.

Finally, programs that use a single stack can often be written more clearly as recursive programs which don't use a stack. (Programs that use two or more stacks, however, often cannot be rewritten as recursive programs without any stacks; but the proof is beyond the scope of this manuscript.)

1.7 WHEN NOT TO USE RECURSION

Every recursive call uses additional memory. The current values of the parameters and other variables at every level must be kept in storage. Modern computers have enough memory that this is usually not an issue—but it can be.

Most programming languages will simply let a recursion run until memory is exhausted, at which point the program will crash. Python, however, sets an arbitrary, but very reasonable, maximum recursion depth of 1000.

> **Note:** Python's depth limit can be changed by calling
> sys.setrecursionlimit(*limit*).

Most recursively defined data structures are nowhere near this deep. For example, a balanced binary tree containing one billion nodes would only be about 30 levels deep.

Lists, like arrays, may have thousands of elements. For these, a method that recurs for every element may be impractical, and a less storage-intensive loop should be used.

1.8 THE FOUR RULES

Here we propose four rules which, if understood and followed, will result in working recursive programs. Once you become comfortable with recursion you will realize that these rules are not absolute, and can be violated for good cause, if care is taken; but stick with them for now.

1. Handle the base cases first.

2. Only recur with a simpler case.

3. Don't use external variables.

4. Don't look down.

1.8.1 Rule 1. Handle the Base Cases First

A **base case** is a task that can be computed directly with no need for recursion. For example, in the factorial program, the only base case is n == 0, and the result returned is 1. Other programs may have multiple base cases, each directly computable. The first thing any recursive program should do is test for base cases.

Often there is a choice between using recursion and using a loop. If efficiency is critical, a loop is usually the better choice. Otherwise, the simpler alternative should be chosen.

The purpose of a base case isn't to avoid recursion altogether. The purpose of a base case is to *stop* a recursion. That brings us to the second rule.

1.8.2 Rule 2. Recur Only with a Simpler Case

This rule is crucial for preventing circularity and infinite recursion. If you ever, even once, recur with the same (or harder) problem, your program immediately disappears off into Cloud-Cuckoo Land.

Every recursive call should be with a simpler case of the same kind of problem. But what does it mean to be "simpler"? If the problem is numeric and the base case is zero, then simpler may mean with a smaller number. If the problem is processing an array, simpler might mean with a smaller array, or a smaller part of an array. Simpler might mean a more nearly sorted array, a shorter arithmetic expression, a shorter list, or just about anything else, so long as it is in some way "closer" to a base case.

In addition, the solution of the simpler case must also be useful in solving the harder case. For example, 10! can be computed by solving the simpler case of 9! and then multiplying this result by 10. To evaluate the expression 3 * (2 + 4), it is first necessary to evaluate the subexpression (2 + 4).

Once you have established your base cases, those are the "simplest" cases, and "simpler" is anything that is in some clear way "closer" to one or more of those base cases. Sometimes it is obvious when we are getting closer, as in the factorial function: As long as n is greater than 0, clearly n − 1 is closer to 0. Similarly, when we evaluate expressions, it may be obvious that a shorter expression is a simpler one; or perhaps it is an expression with fewer parentheses, or fewer arithmetic operators. When you write a recursive function, *you* must be clear in your mind just when a problem is "closer" to the base case (hence "simpler"), and you must stick to it.

Suppose we try to speed up the factorial function by doing two multiplications at each level of recursion, rather than just one. We might get

```python
def bad_factorial(n):
    if n == 0:
        return 1
    else:
        return n * (n - 1) * bad_factorial(n - 2)
```

Or in Java:

```java
public static int badFactorial(int n) {
    if (n == 0) return 1;
    else return n * (n - 1) * factorial(n - 2);
}
```

This doesn't work. Before you read any further, try to figure out the error for yourself. Then figure out the simple fix.

The problem is that n - 2 isn't necessarily "closer" to 0 than n is. In particular, if n is odd, so is n - 2, and soon we will overshoot 0 and try to compute the factorials of -1,-3,-5, and so on. It is part of the notion of "closer" that (in a finite system), if we get closer enough times, sooner or later we will get there. (This can be corrected by changing the test to if n == 0 or n == 1.)

So you have to be careful that your notion of "closer" will sooner or later get you there.

If this all sounds vague and mysterious, don't panic. For any particular, concrete problem, it is 99% certain that it will be obvious what meaning to attach to the word "simpler." But *do* take 20 seconds, before you rush ahead with the program, to decide what the word means. Then each time you write a recursive call, make sure you recur with a simpler problem.

1.8.2.1 An Aside: The Collatz Conjecture

It is almost always easy to determine whether a recursive case is closer to the base case. However, the **Collatz conjecture** is a rare counterexample. In Python,

```python
def collatz(n):
    if n == 1:
        return 1
```

```
    elif n % 2 == 0:
        return collatz(n // 2) # integer division
    else:
        return collatz(3 * n + 1)
```

The conjecture is that the collatz function will terminate for all positive integers. There is only one base case: If n is 1, the result is one. Therefore, if the function does terminate, the result will be 1.

Does it terminate? If n is even, collatz is called with half of n, which is closer to 1. But if n is odd, collatz is called with 3 * n + 1, which is larger than n but even, so the parameter will come down again, just not as far.

The Collatz conjecture has mathematicians stumped. It has been checked by computer programs for all values up to 2^{68}, and always terminates. There must be some measure by which both n/2 and 3n + 1 are "closer" to one, but it obviously isn't just the size of the number. A mathematical proof of termination has yet to be discovered.

1.8.3 Rule 3. Don't Use External Variables

Local variables are variables that can only be used inside the function in which they are defined; they are inaccessible outside the function. But it goes deeper than that. Local variables can only be used in one particular instantiation (call) of a function. If the function is called again, it uses a whole new set of local variables.

Suppose you have two functions, A and B. If function A calls function B, here's what happens:

1. When A calls B, all the local variables of A are tucked away in a safe place, inaccessible to B (or anything else).

2. If A calls B with arguments, the values of those arguments are copied into B's parameters.

3. New storage locations are allocated for all the local variables of B, including the variables in B's parameter list. This storage allocation may happen immediately, or it may happen as needed by function B.

4. Function B executes its code, using the values in its new storage locations. When done, function B returns a single result to A, and all storage used by all the local variables of B is recycled.

5. When A receives a result from B, all its local variables are brought "out of hiding," still with the same values they had when B was called.

Here's the key point: *All those same actions occur when a function calls itself.* The local variable names are reused for the new values, and their previous values are restored when the call returns.

Global variables are different. Consider the following sequence:

1. Compute a value for x,

2. make a recursive call,

3. use x, expecting it to have the value you computed in (1).

If x is a local variable, there is no problem. Variable x will not be changed by the recursive call. But if x is a global variable, it *will* be changed by the recursive call. Step (1) above changes it.

Local variables don't cause any problems. They just don't. They are safe from whatever happens at other levels of the recursion.

However, if a recursive routine uses and modifies an external variable, such as a global, then you can only understand and debug the routine by understanding how the *calling* routine manipulates the variable *and also* how the *called* routine manipulates the variable. This requires you to think about many levels of the recursive routine, all at the same time. For most programmers (and possibly all programmers), this is impossible.

There are two ways in which you can safely use an external variable in a recursive routine:

- Never change the value of an external variable, only look at it; or,

- Never use the value of an external variable, only change it (a counter, for example).

This doesn't mean that you *cannot* both use and change a global variable in a recursive method; you can, but it becomes very difficult to reason about.

It is helpful to understand that a variable can only hold a limited amount of information, typically four bytes (depending on the system). Four bytes is enough to hold quite large integers, floating point numbers, booleans, and pointers, but it isn't enough to hold complex values like arrays, lists, sets, tuples, or dictionaries. These larger structures are stored elsewhere, and a pointer to them is stored in the variable.

A recursive routine thus may access four types of variables:

1. Local variables, which are declared inside the routine itself, and are totally safe.

2. Parameters that are "passed by value," that is, the actual value of the argument can fit in a single variable, and it is

this value which is copied into the parameter. Such parameters act like local variables.

3. Global variables, which are external to the routine. Any change to a global variable is visible everywhere. It is safe to only look at them, and it is safe to only update them (for example, incrementing a counter), but trying to work with them in any meaningful way will quickly lead to incomprehensible code.

4. Parameters that are "passed by reference." Arrays, lists, and other data structures cannot fit in a single variable, so what is copied into the parameter is a *reference* (or *pointer*) to the actual value. These behave like global variables.

Moral: Make sure *all* your variables are either local or are by-value parameters. If you can't, make sure you never change the value of a global variable or parameter. And if you must alter global variables, think long and hard about what you're doing.

Technical Note: Starting in Python 3, integers can be of unlimited size. A variable holding a very large integer would normally hold a reference, rather than the actual value. However, large numbers are immutable, so integers continue to behave as they have always done, regardless of how large they are.

Fortunately, it is easy to get into the habit of avoiding globals. You don't have to think through the reasons each time. Just avoid them.

1.8.3.1 Deep Copies

You never need a complex data structure to be a global variable; it can always be passed around as a parameter. Doing so is efficient because what you are actually passing is a reference (pointer) to the data structure.

Modifying a data structure within a recursive function has the same problems as modifying a global variable. Since what you have is a reference to the data structure, any modifications to it happen at all levels of the recursion.

Sometimes the whole point of the recursive function is to modify the data structure. In this case, a simpler case (Rule 2) is usually to use just part of the data structure.

Other times, a data structure might be modified on a trial-and-error basis, for example when searching for a solution, after which the changes must be undone. Undoing changes can be efficient but error-prone. Another approach is to pass a copy of the data structure rather than the original; the entire copy can be discarded when the function returns, leaving the original untouched.

Copies can be *shallow* or *deep*. A **shallow copy** is a simple copy of all the top-level values in the data structure. For example, consider the following Python array:

```
a = [1, [2, 3], 4]
```

(Python calls this a list, but it's actually more like an array.) The variable a now holds a reference to the array. If we do a simple assignment, b = a, the *reference* is copied into b, so that now a and b both refer to the same array. Again, it is the reference that is copied, not the actual array. The same thing happens when a is passed to b as a parameter.

```
b = a
b[0] = 10
b[1][0] = 20
print(a) # prints [10, [20, 3], 4]
```

Python has a copy method. The array a has three values: the integer 1, a *reference to* the array [2, 3], and the integer 4. When the array itself is copied, these three values are the ones that are copied into the new array.

```
b = a.copy()
b[0] = 10
b[1][0] = 20
print(a) # prints [1, [20, 3], 4]
```

The value 1 in array a was not changed, but the value 2 was changed to 20. This happened because only the reference to the array [2, 3] was copied, not the complete array. A *deep copy*, on the other hand, copies the entire structure.

```
import copy
a = [1, [2, 3], 4]
b = copy.deepcopy(a)
b[0] = 10
b[1][0] = 20
print(a) # prints [1, [2, 3], 4]
```

Copying a data structure can be expensive, and deep copying even more expensive, but if you must make tentative modifications to a data structure in a recursive function, you may need to work on a copy.

1.8.4 Rule 4. Don't Look Down

When you reach a recursive call, *don't* go back to the top of your routine and start working through it all over again. Don't try to "trace through" recursive calls. That way lies madness.

Consider this: if you are working your way through a complex but non-recursive routine, and it calls a sorting routine, do you drop everything and rush off to see if the sorting routine works? Of course not. You simply assume that the sorting routine works (if you have doubts you save them for later), and keep going in the routine you're checking. Rule 4 simply says to treat *all* calls this way, even recursive ones.

It may seem odd at first to assume the called routine works, when that called routine happens to be the very one you're checking. However, you must do so: the human mind does have limitations. Pretend, if it helps, that you are not actually recurring, but rather calling an entirely different routine (which happens to have the same name) that you know to be correct.

What is involved here is perhaps best described as a "leap of faith." You have to learn to trust recursion; to believe that, if you can get the routine correct *at this level*, then you don't have to worry about any deeper levels. Until you can bring yourself to make this commitment, you will be compelled to look down into the recursion, and you will never untangle what you see there.

Think about rules one to three, and try to convince yourself logically that a program written according to these rules ought to work. Then, even if you can't yet manage rule four, pretend you do when you write your program.

Now run your program. It will have errors, of course—programs always do—but steadfastly refuse to look down. Go over rules one, two, and three, and make sure you didn't violate one of these. Next, go over the program the same way you always would, looking for errors that have nothing to do with the recursion itself (the error doesn't *have* to be in the recursion, remember). If this too fails, get help.

Don't even think about looking down, for this one simple reason: it doesn't help.

If the notion of "faith" bothers you, think about the novice programmer who complains that his program can't be wrong, so the computer must have made a mistake. You may have once done this yourself. In time, all programmers learn to trust the computer; now you must learn to trust recursion.

1.9 WHAT THE COMPUTER DOES

This section is optional; feel free to skip it.

Here's the factorial function again.

```
def factorial(n):
    if n == 0:
        return 1
    else:
        return factorial(n - 1) * n
```

Suppose the program calls factorial with 3. What happens?

1. The value 3 is assigned to the local variable n.

   • n is not zero, so the function "remembers" that n is 3, (it puts 3 on a stack) and calls factorial with 2.

2. The value 2 is assigned to the local variable n.

   • n is not zero, so the function puts 2 on a stack and calls factorial with 1.

3. The value 1 is assigned to the local variable n.

   • n is not zero, so the function puts 1 on a stack and calls factorial with 0.

4. The value 0 is assigned to the local variable n.

   • n is zero, so the function returns 1.

5. The function pops the 1 from the stack (it was put on the stack in step 3).

   • The function multiplies the 1 from the function call by the 1 from the stack, and returns 1.

6. The function pops the 2 from the stack (it was put on the stack in step 2).

- The function multiplies the 1 from the function call by the 2 from the stack, and returns 2.

7. The function pops the 3 from the stack (it was put on the stack in step 1).

- The function multiplies the 2 from the function call by the 3 from the stack, and returns 6.

8. The function returns with 6 as the final result.

According to many textbooks, this is how you are supposed to understand recursion. It doesn't work for me, and it probably doesn't work for you.

1.10 REMOVING RECURSION

As has been mentioned, recursion is never necessary; anything that can be done with recursion can also be done using stacks and loops.

A **stack** is a *first-in last-out* data structure. That is, values can be added to the stack, and they can be taken from the stack, but they will be removed in the opposite order from which they were added. Think of a stack of books—you can add a book to the top of the stack, or take a book from the top of the stack. If you put several books onto a stack, the first book will be at the bottom of the stack, and it will be the last book you can get to.

Java has a Stack class. Python doesn't, but Python lists can be used like stacks. Here are the basic operations in the Java Stack class, along with the equivalent list operations in Python.

- **stack**.push(**value**)—adds **value** to the stack. In Python, use **list**.append(**value**).

- **stack**.pop()—removes and returns the top value. In Python, use **list**.pop().

- ***stack***.peek()—returns the top value of the stack but does not remove it. In Python, use ***list*** [-1].

- ***stack***.empty()—tests if the stack is empty. In Python, use ***list*** == [].

The way recursion is implemented "under the hood" is fairly simple. All local values are pushed onto a stack when the recursive call is made and restored from the stack when the call returns. This can be simulated with a loop, exiting the loop when the base case is reached.

Here again is the recursive version:

```
def r_factorial(n):
    """Compute the factorial of its argument."""
    if n == 0:
        return 1
    else:
        return r_factorial(n - 1) * n
```

And here is a version that uses a stack to simulate recursion:

```
def factorial(n):
    """Compute the factorial of its argument."""
    stack = []
    while n != 0:
        stack.append(n) # "push"
        n = n - 1
    fac = 1
    while stack != []:
        n = stack.pop()
        fac = fac * n
    return fac
```

In the non-recursive version, putting n on the stack and setting n to n - 1 is the equivalent of saving the local variable n and making a recursive call with n − 1. Popping the stack and putting the top value back in n is the equivalent of returning from a recursive call.

Clearly, the recursive version factorial is simpler; the point is to show that recursion can be implemented by using a stack. The main reason one might wish to do so is that recursion, especially very deep recursion (thousands of levels), can be computationally expensive, due to the amount of space required by the stack.

1.11 TAIL RECURSION

A function is *tail recursive* if the recursion is the very last thing done in the function. If the function contains more than one recursive call, it is tail recursive if every recursive call is the last operation in the function.

Consider, once more, the factorial function.

```
def factorial(n):
    """Compute the factorial of its argument."""
    if n == 0:
        return 1
    else:
        return factorial(n - 1) * n
```

This function is *not* tail recursive. The recursive call occurs in the last statement of the function, but it is not the last thing done; after the recursive call, the result of that call is multiplied by n.

The factorial function can be made tail-recursive by pulling the multiplication into an extra parameter (an *accumulator*) and providing a user-facing function (a *façade*) to call it. This is a technique that will be discussed in more detail later. For the present, here is the code.

```
def factorial(n):
    return fac(n, 1)

def fac(n, acc):
    if n == 0:
        return acc
    else:
        return fac(n - 1, n * acc)
```

In a recursive function, every call gives you a new set of local variables. The advantage of tail recursion is that local variables are not used again after the recursive call. Because they are not used again, there is no need to create a new set; the existing variables can be reused. This makes it much simpler to replace the recursion with a loop.

```
def factorial(n):
    acc = 1
    while n != 0:
        acc = n * acc
        n = n - 1
    return acc
```

Some languages, such as Scala, are sometimes able to detect tail recursion and perform this optimization by themselves. For other languages, including Python and Java, it is up to the programmer to do the optimization manually.

1.12 RECURSIVE DRAWINGS

No description of recursion would be complete without at least a mention of *recursive drawings*.

As an example, draw a square. At each corner of the square, draw a square half as large, centered at that corner. For each of those squares, draw squares half as large, centered at each of the corners of those squares. Continue until the squares get too small. The result will look something like Figure 1.1.

FIGURE 1.1   Recursive squares.

Recursive drawings can be made in both Python and Java, but it's a lot of work. The Processing "language" is basically a layer on top of either Python or Java that provides very nice drawing tools.

Here is a program to make the above drawing in Processing, using Python syntax:

```
size(400, 400)
background(255)
rectMode(CENTER)
noFill()
```

```
def squares(x, y, size):
    if size < 12:
        return
    square(x, y, size)
    half = size / 2
    squares(x - half, y - half, half)
    squares(x + half, y - half, half)
    squares(x - half, y + half, half)
    squares(x + half, y + half, half)

squares(200, 200, 175)
```

(The built-in square method is the one that does the actual drawing.) Here is the same program in Java:

```
public void settings() {
    size(400, 400);
}
void squares(int x, int y, int size) {
    if (size < 12) return;
    square(x, y, size);
    int half = size / 2;
    squares(x - half, y - half, half);
    squares(x + half, y - half, half);
    squares(x - half, y + half, half);
    squares(x + half, y + half, half);
}

void draw() {
    background(255);
    rectMode(CENTER);
    noFill();
    squares(200, 200, 175);
}
```

1.13 FORTRAN AND LISP

The two most important programming languages from the 1950s, Fortran and Lisp, are still in use, although they have evolved considerably. Both have had an immense influence on the programming languages we use today. It can be argued that modern, conventional languages are structurally most like Fortran, but incorporate most of the ideas from Lisp.

Fortran was used for numerical processing; it was built around numbers, arrays, and loops. Early versions had no symbols or lists and did not support recursion.

Lisp was used for nonnumerical processing (in particular, what we today would call "artificial intelligence" applications). It was built around lists, symbols, and recursion. It had numbers (awkwardly) but not arrays or loops.

It should therefore be no surprise that, while recursion can sometimes be useful for dealing with arrays, it is far more important in working with lists and other recursively defined data structures.

CHAPTER 2

Data Structures

2.1 ARRAYS

An **array** is a sequence of values, all of the same data type, stored in contiguous memory locations. Any element can be efficiently accessed by its **index** in the array. In most languages, the minimum index is zero and the maximum index is the size of the array minus one.

2.1.1 Array Maximum

This time we will devise a recursive Python program to find the maximum value in an array. Again, it would be better to do this without recursion, but it is difficult to find simple examples that really need recursion, at least until we have discussed some recursively defined data structures.

When looking for the maximum value in a nonempty array, what is a simpler problem of the same sort? Obviously, finding the maximum of a smaller array. So we will plan to recur only with smaller arrays, and our base case will be the smallest array—that is, an array of only one element.

DOI: 10.1201/9781003359616-2

Here is one approach: Take a number from one end of the array; recursively find the maximum of the remaining array; compare the maximum to the one number taken, and the maximum is the larger of these. For a base case, the maximum of a single-element array is that element.

While this approach is workable, it isn't very interesting. Here's an approach I like better: Divide the array (approximately) in half; recursively find the maximum of each half; return the larger of these two maxima as the grand maximum. Again, the base case is a one-element array, with that one element as the maximum.

This logic translates easily into Python code.

```python
def maximum(numbers):
    """Find the maximum value in list 'numbers'."""
    if len(numbers) == 1:
        return numbers[0]
    mid = len(numbers) // 2 # integer division
    leftmax = maximum(numbers[0:mid])
    rightmax = maximum(numbers[mid:len(numbers)])
    if leftmax > rightmax:
        return leftmax
    else:
        return rightmax
```

Note: Array slicing (the [mid:len] syntax) makes a copy of that part of the array, so the above function is much less efficient than it might appear.

The same algorithm isn't quite as easy in Java, which does not support passing in part of an array as an argument. Instead, we use a helper method that takes two additional arguments, the lower bound and the upper bound of an interval in the array. No copying is involved, so this will be much more efficient than the Python version.

```
public static int maximum(int[] numbers) {
    return maxHelper(numbers, 0, numbers.length - 1);
}

private static int maxHelper(int[] numbers,
                            int lo, int hi) {
    if (lo == hi) return numbers[lo];
    int mid = (lo + hi) / 2;
    int leftmax = maxHelper(numbers, lo, mid);
    int rightmax = maxHelper(numbers, mid + 1, hi);
    if (leftmax > rightmax) return leftmax;
    else return rightmax;
}
```

Do these programs satisfy the four rules?

1. Do they handle the base case(s) first? Yes, if there is only one number in the array interval, that number is returned.

2. Do they recur only with a simpler case? Yes, there are two recursions, each with either a smaller array or an array interval of size 1.

3. Do they have side effects that interfere with the calling program? No, because every variable is local, and the numbers list or array is not changed.

4. Do we need to "look down" into the recursion, or otherwise consider what is happening at some other level? No, we don't.

And we're done.

2.1.2 Quicksort

Quicksort is one of the most widely used sorting algorithms, and it is inherently recursive.

Quicksort was invented by one of the programming greats, Tony Hoare. At the time he was unable to implement the algorithm in Autocode, which did not support recursion. When attending a course on Algol 60, one of the first programming languages (after Lisp) to support recursion, he was able to do so.

The trickiest part of writing a quicksort algorithm is not the recursive part, but is instead a nonrecursive method, usually called partition, that it uses.

The partition method takes three parameters: an array, a smallest index, and a largest index. Then, the partition method:

1. chooses any number from within the given array interval (often the first number, because that's easy), and uses this number as the *pivot*;

2. rearranges the numbers in the array interval so that the numbers less than the pivot precede all the numbers larger than the pivot, and the pivot is in between the two groups (numbers equal to the pivot may be in either group); and

3. returns the index at which the pivot value ended up.

For example, given the array

[5, 7, 1, 9, 8, 2, 3, 2, 9, 4, 5, 1, 3]

the partition method might choose 5 as the pivot, produce the array

[2, 3, 1, 1, 4, 2, 3, 5, 9, 8, 5, 9, 7]

and return 7 as the index of the pivot.

In this example, all the numbers less than 5 are to the left of the pivot (the first 5), and all the numbers greater than 5 are to the right of the pivot. (Another 5 happened to end up to the right of the pivot.) Note that the array is not yet sorted, merely divided into numbers less than or equal to the pivot and numbers greater than or equal to the pivot.

As mentioned, the code for partition tends to be difficult to program correctly. Since partition is not itself recursive, we will leave the actual code to Appendix A for Java and Appendix B for Python.

Here is the code for quicksort, first in Python:

```python
def quicksort(array, left, right):
    if left < right:
        p = partition(array, left, right)
        quicksort(array, left, p - 1)
        quicksort(array, p + 1, right)
```

then in Java:

```java
public static void quicksort(int[] array,
                             int left,
                             int right) {
    if (left < right) {
        int p = partition(array, left, right);
        quicksort(array, left, p - 1);
        quicksort(array, p + 1, right);
    }
}
```

Is this a correct recursion?

- The base case is when left is greater than or equal to right. There is nothing more to do, and quicksort terminates.

- Each recursive call is with a smaller part of the array, so the difference right - left decreases until it becomes zero or negative.

- The methods are self-contained, using no global variables.

- quicksort uses another method, partition. The programmer must understand what this method does, but understanding how it works is irrelevant to understanding quicksort itself.

Here's a call to quicksort in Python:

```
quicksort(array, 0, len(array) - 1)
```

Here's a call to quicksort in Java:

```
Quicksort.quicksort(array, 0, array.length - 1);
```

Finally, it should be noted that, while quicksort is extremely fast *on average,* it can be inefficient in some cases. Unfortunately, a worst case occurs when it is applied to an array that is already sorted. Many of the various modifications to quicksort are an attempt to deal with this problem.

2.2 LISTS

A *list* is either empty, or it has a *head* (a first element) and a *tail* (a list of all the remaining elements). This is a recursive definition with the empty list serving as a base case.

The elements of a list may be a value of any sort, including other lists. This allows for some fairly complex structures to be built.

Every list must come to an end, and that occurs when the tail is the empty list. An empty list can be represented by the value null (in Java) or None (in Python).

There are only a very few basic operations on a list. They are as follows:

- Test if the list is empty.

- Get the head of a nonempty list.

- Get the tail of a nonempty list.

- Construct a new list with a given head and a given tail.

2.2.1 Lists in Java

Recursion is best demonstrated using singly linked lists, which Java does not provide. The practical programmer should use Java's more complex lists, but for instructional purposes we will implement and use a simple singly linked list class.

Here's all the code needed for a basic implementation of a list type (in Java):

```java
public class List {
    public Object head;
    public List tail;

    public List(Object head, List tail) {
        this.head = head;
        this.tail = tail;
    }
}
```

The above code includes a constructor and provides direct access to the head and the tail. To test if a list is empty, test if it is equal to null. To test if something is a (nonempty) list, use Java's instanceof operator.

Almost all list algorithms follow the same mantra: **Do something with the head and recur with the tail**, stopping when the list is empty. This is a special case of the usual approach to recursion: An empty list is a base case, and the tail of a list is simpler than the entire list.

One of the things we might want to do with lists is to test whether two lists are equal, that is, they have equal elements in the same order. Conceptually, this is very easy: Two lists are equal if their heads are equal and their tails are equal. As is frequently the case in Java, the need to check for null greatly complicates the code. The head of a list may be null because it contains an empty list as a member. The tail of a list will be null if the element is the last thing in the list. Any expression of the form x.equals(y) will be in error if x could possibly be null.

It is surprisingly difficult to write a single equals method for lists, but pulling the null tests into a separate function (eq) results in readable code.

```
@Override
public boolean equals(Object obj) {
    if (! (obj instanceof List)) return false;
    List that = (List) obj;
    return eq(this.head, that.head) &&
        eq(this.tail, that.tail);
}
```

Java requires that the parameter to equals be of type Object. Therefore, we must next check the type of the parameter obj, and return false if it isn't a List. Then we can use a cast to save obj in variable that of type List. Once the bureaucracy is satisfied, the actual work is done in the return statement.

The helper function eq can be used to avoid nullPointer-Exceptions with any types of objects, using the equals method defined for obj1.

```
private static boolean eq(Object obj1, Object obj2) {
    if (obj1 == null) return obj2 == null;
    return obj1.equals(obj2);
}
```

Another important operation is to test whether a given value is a member of a list. The method eq can again be used as a helper method.

```
public static boolean member(Object obj, List lst) {
    if (lst == null) return false;
    if (eq(obj, lst.head)) return true;
    return member(obj, lst.tail);
}
```

The member method tests whether a value is a top-level member of a list. If we want to know whether a value exists anywhere in a list, possibly in a sublist or sub-sublist, we need a slightly more complex method.

```
public static boolean deepMember(Object obj, List lst) {
    if (lst == null) return false;
    if (eq(obj, lst.head)) return true;
    if (lst.head instanceof List &&
        deepMember(obj, (List) lst.head)) return true;
    return deepMember(obj, lst.tail);
}
```

2.2.2 Lists in Python

According to the usual definition, a *singly linked list* (or briefly, *list*) is a linear data structure that has a *head* (first element) and a *tail* (all the remaining elements, in some order). Access to these two values, the head and the tail, is very efficient; access to any other values involves stepping through the intervening values to get to them.

Python has a data structure called a "list," but it is actually a complex data structure that has features of both arrays and lists.

This is convenient for many applications, but using it as if it were a singly linked list would be inefficient, and therefore inadvisable.

It is easy to write a List class in Python that has the usual characteristics of a singly linked list. Such a class could begin like this:

```
class List:
    def __init__(self, head, tail=None):
        """Construct a List."""
        self.head = head
        self.tail = tail
```

As a first example of using the List class, we will count the number of elements in a list, using the aforementioned mantra, "Do something with the head and recur with the tail." In this case, what we do with the head is simply count it.

```
def length(lst):
    """Count the top-level elements in a List."""
    if lst == None:
        return 0
    return 1 + length(lst.tail)
```

In order to print a list, we will need a method to represent it as a string. Here is an implementation of the __str__ method, as it would occur inside the List class.

```
def __str__(self):
    """Return a string representation
        of this List."""
    return '[' + self.contents() + ']'

def contents(self):
    """Return a string representation of
        the contents of this List."""
    s = str(self.head)
```

```
if self.tail != None:
    s += ', ' + self.tail.contents()
return s
```

In this code, only the helper method contents is recursive; the __str__ method simply add brackets around the result.

Additional list methods in Python (equality testing, member, deepMember) are provided in Appendix K.

2.2.3 Accumulators

It's easy to copy a list recursively; simply make a new list with a copy of the head and a copy of the tail.

```
def list_copy(lst):
    if lst == None:
        return None
    return List(lst.head, list_copy(lst.tail))
```

The above code makes a shallow copy, which is adequate for the purposes of this section.

Now consider the problem of creating a new list containing the same elements as a given list, but in reverse order. One way to do this is to use an *accumulator:* an additional parameter that incrementally builds, or accumulates, the final result.

The user of the reverse method should not have to know about the accumulator, and certainly should not have to provide one in the correct form. Hence we provide a façade method that takes a single list parameter and calls another function to do the actual work.

```
def reverse(self):
    return self.rev(self, None)
```

```
def rev(self, lst, acc=None):
    if lst == None:
        return acc
    return lst.rev(lst.tail,
                    List(lst.head, acc))
```

Each call of rev plucks an item from the original list (lst.head), adds it to the list being accumulated (List(lst.head, acc)), and recurs with the shorter original list (lst.tail) and the list being accumulated. When all the elements of the original list have been processed (lst == None), the complete reversed list is in acc.

This follows the conventional method for a recursive list method: Handle the base case (lst == None) first, then do something with the head and recur with the tail. The accumulator is simply another variable that goes along for the ride.

The Java code is similar. Since Java allows methods to be **overloaded** (multiple methods may have the same name if the parameter lists are different), we can use the same name for both the façade method and the main method.

```
public List reverse() {
    return reverse(this, null);
}

private List reverse(List lst, List acc) {
    if (lst == null) return acc;
    return reverse(lst.tail,
            new List(lst.head, acc));
}
```

2.3 BINARY TREES

We will define a **binary tree** (Figure 2.1) as either empty or consisting of a **root node** (object) that contains three parts:

- A value, which could be anything,

- A *left child*, which is a binary tree; and

- A *right child*, which is a binary tree.

Binary trees are defined recursively: A (non-empty) binary tree consists of a value and two other binary trees. The values in each node are the user data, while the (references to) other binary trees provide the structure.

> **Note:** Yes, this definition allows a binary tree to be empty (null or None). This lets us think of a node as always having two children, one or both of which may be empty, and this simplifies programming. In mathematics, an empty binary tree would be called a *degenerate case*.

All nodes are reachable (by one or more steps) from the root node. In general, it is only possible to move "down" in the binary tree (from parent to child), not "up" (from child to parent). A node that has neither a left child nor a right child is called a *leaf* and is used as the base case in many applications.

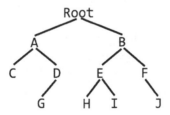

FIGURE 2.1   A binary tree.

There are some other constraints that a binary tree must satisfy. A binary tree is not allowed to contain cycles; that is, a node may not have one of its own ancestors as a child. In addition, some (but not all) implementations insist that each node except the root has exactly one parent; this prevents having **shared subtrees,** in which there may be more than one path from the root to a given node. Other implementations may have other kinds of constraints.

Checking these constraints is complicated. Library implementations of binary trees must do all this work, but it isn't needed here. In this book, we need only the simplest implementations to illustrate recursive techniques.

Here's a definition of a BinaryTree class in Java:

```java
public class BinaryTree {
    public Object value;
    BinaryTree left = null;
    BinaryTree right = null;

    BinaryTree(Object value,
        BinaryTree left,
        BinaryTree right) {
    this.value = value;
    this.left = left;
    this.right = right;
    }

    BinaryTree(Object value) {
        // shortcut for making a leaf
        this(value, null, null);
        }
    }
```

As defined above, the "value" in each node is type String. To make a more general binary tree, it could be Object. Even better, this class could be genericized, so that the binary tree could contain values of only some designated type. Our goal here, however, is to keep things simple, and that means ignoring generics.

Here's the equivalent code in Python.

```python
class BinaryTree(object):
    def __init__(self, value, left=None, right=None):
        self.value = value
        self.left = left
        self.right = right
```

With these constructors, trees have to be built from the bottom up. To construct a node, its child nodes must already have been defined. The example tree given above can be constructed like this:

In Java:

```java
static BinaryTree makeTree() {
    BinaryTree root, a, b, c, d, e, f, g, h, i, j;
    g = new BinaryTree("G");
    h = new BinaryTree("H");
    i = new BinaryTree("I");
    j = new BinaryTree("J");
    c = new BinaryTree("C");
    d = new BinaryTree("D", g, null);
    e = new BinaryTree("E", h, i);
    f = new BinaryTree("F", null, j);
    a = new BinaryTree("A", c, d);
    b = new BinaryTree("B", e, f);
    return new BinaryTree("Root", a, b);
}
```

And in Python:

```python
def make_tree():
    g = BinaryTree('G')
    h = BinaryTree('H')
    i = BinaryTree('I')
    j = BinaryTree('J')
    c = BinaryTree('C')
    d = BinaryTree('D', g, None)
```

```
e = BinaryTree('E', h, i)
f = BinaryTree('F', None, j)
a = BinaryTree('A', c, d)
b = BinaryTree('B', e, f)
return BinaryTree('Root', a, b)
```

Binary trees will be used in a later section. Meanwhile, let's examine some recursive routines for manipulating binary trees.

2.3.1 Printing Binary Trees

Suppose we want to print a binary tree. Neither Java nor Python can print our binary trees in a useful fashion without some assistance. In Java, we will need to override the toString method; in Python we need to supply a __str__ method.

One reasonable way to print a binary tree is this:

- If a node has children, print its value; then, in parentheses, print its left subtree and its right subtree. Print "null" or "None" for a missing subtree.

- If a node is a leaf, just print its value.

With this approach, the example binary tree would print as

```
Root(A(C, D(G, null)), B(E(H, I), F(null, J)))
```

in Java, and

```
Root(A(C, D(G, None)), B(E(H, I), F(None, J)))
```

in Python. In both cases, the code is very simple. In Java,

```
@Override
public String toString() {
    if (left == null && right == null) {
        return value.toString();
```

```
    }
    return value + "(" + left + ", " + right + ")";
}
```

and in Python,

```python
def __str__(self):
    if (self.left == None and
        self.right == None):
        return str(self.value)
    return (str(self.value) + "(" +
            str(self.left) + ", " +
            str(self.right) + ")")
```

Are there base cases? Yes, whenever we reach a leaf, we don't recur.

Is each recursion simpler, that is, nearer a base case? Yes, each recursive call is with a child of the current node, so each recursive call is closer to the leaves. There is a caveat, however. A well-formed binary tree has no cycles; no node has a child that is also one of its ancestors. If this condition is violated, an infinite recursion will result.

Are globals used? No, each method is self-contained.

We can conclude from this that the recursive logic is correct. That does not, of course, guarantee that the implementation will be free of bugs; testing is still required.

2.3.2 Counting Nodes
As another quick example, we wish to count the nodes in a binary tree.

Any node in a binary tree may be regarded as the root of a binary tree. From any node, its parent (if it has one) is not accessible. Therefore we can think of any node in a binary tree as being a

root node with two **subtrees**, a left subtree and a right subtree.
The number of nodes in a binary tree is therefore 1 (the root
node), plus the number of nodes in its left subtree, plus the
number of nodes in its right subtree.

A first cut at the node-counting method is therefore (in Python):

```
def count_nodes(bt):
    return (1
            + count_nodes(bt.left)
            + count_nodes(bt.right)
```

This isn't quite right. It does work its way "down" the binary tree
toward the leaves, but what happens once it gets there? There is
no base case.

We can make this complicated. We can say: If a node has no
right child and no left child, then it's a leaf, so count it as 1 and
don't recur. If it has only a left child, then add 1 to the result and
recur on the left child. If it has only a right child, then add 1 to
the result and recur on the right child. This would work.

There is a much simpler approach. By our definition, a binary
tree could be empty, so we can always recur on both the left child
and the right child. If the recursive call is with None (an empty
tree), that tree clearly contains no nodes, and 0 should be the
value returned by the recursion.

Base cases, you will remember, go first.

```
def count_nodes(bt):
    if bt == None:
        return 0
    return (1
            + count_nodes(bt.left)
            + count_nodes(bt.right))
```

The logic is identical for Java.

```java
static int countNodes(BinaryTree bt) {
    if (bt == null) return 0;
    return (1
            + countNodes(bt.left)
            + countNodes(bt.right));
}
```

So the base case is an empty node, the recursive case is always with a smaller subtree, and there are no global variables to cause confusion.

2.4 TREES

Whereas a binary tree consists of a root node containing a value and up to two children, a (general) *tree* consists of a root node containing a value and any number of children.

A BinaryTree class definition starts out like this:

```java
public class BinaryTree {
    public Object value;
    BinaryTree leftChild = null;
    BinaryTree rightChild = null;
    ...
}
```

In contrast, the definition of a Tree class starts out like this:

```java
public class Tree {
    public Object value;
    private ArrayList children;
```

or with generics,

```java
public class Tree<V> {
    public V value;
    private ArrayList<Tree<V>> children;
```

The code is similar in Python.

```python
class Tree:
    def __init__(self, value):
        self.value = value
        self.children = []
```

A Java implementation of a Tree class is provided in Appendix L.

2.4.1 Parse Trees

Every time a program is compiled, in virtually any language, the compiler creates a *parse tree*. This is a tree that represents the structure of a program. For example, the small code fragment

```python
if a > b:
    temp = a
    a = b
    b = temp
```

is turned into a tree somewhat like the one in Figure 2.2.

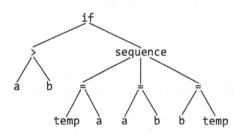

FIGURE 2.2   A parse tree.

This parse tree can then be translated into another language (perhaps assembler), or it could be interpreted directly.

Here is some pseudocode to suggest how that might be done.

```
function interpret(node):
    if node type is "if":
        if (interpret first child):
            interpret second child
        else:
            interpret third child (if present)
    else if node type is [something else]
        [do something else]
```

2.4.2 Indirect Recursion

A recursive method is simply another kind of method. There is nothing unusual about one recursive method calling another.

Earlier we defined a Python method __str__ which is automatically called whenever a List object is to be printed or otherwise converted to a string. Now we can do the same for trees.

```
def __str__(self):
    s = str(self.value)
    if self.children != None:
        s += str(self.children)
    return s
```

This method is not obviously recursive. Given a Tree, it will return a string representation of the value in the root node and, if the root node has children, a string representation of the list of children. However, those children will themselves be Trees. When each child is converted to a string, it will be done by using the __str__ method in the Tree class.

In other words, getting a string representation of a Tree involves calling a method to get a string representation of a list, which involves calling the method to get string representations of Trees. This is an example of ***indirect recursion.***

Does the above method terminate? Although it isn't placed first in the method, the above Tree method does have a base case when self.children == None. Each call works its way down the tree, so the base case will eventually be reached on every branch. If we can assume that stepping through a list terminates, then the procedure as a whole will terminate.

CHAPTER 3

Backtracking

BACKTRACKING IS A FORM of recursion.

The usual scenario is that you are faced with a number of options, and you must choose one of these. After you make your choice you will get a new set of options; just what set of options you get depends on what choice you made. This procedure is repeated over and over until you reach a final state. If you made a good sequence of choices, your final state is a goal state; if you didn't, it isn't.

Conceptually, you start at the root of a tree; the tree probably has some good leaves and some bad leaves, though it may be that the leaves are all good or all bad. You want to get to a good leaf. At each node, beginning with the root, you choose one of its children to move to, and you keep this up until you get to a leaf.

Suppose you get to a bad leaf. You can backtrack to continue the search for a good leaf by revoking your most recent choice and trying out the next option in that set of options. If you run out of options, revoke the choice that got you here, and try another choice at that node. If you end up at the root with no options left, there are no good leaves to be found.

DOI: 10.1201/9781003359616-3

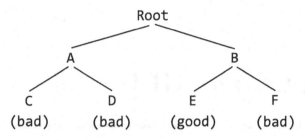

FIGURE 3.1   A tree with one good leaf.

The following shows how backtracking might proceed on the tree in Figure 3.1:

1. Starting at Root, your options are A and B. You choose A.

2. At A, your options are C and D. You choose C.

3. C is bad. Go back to A.

4. At A, you have already tried C, and it failed. Try D.

5. D is bad. Go back to A.

6. At A, you have no options left to try. Go back to Root.

7. At Root, you have already tried A. Try B.

8. At B, your options are E and F. Try E.

9. E is good. Congratulations!

In this example we drew a picture of a tree. The tree is an abstract model of the possible sequences of choices we could make. There is also a data structure called a tree, but sometimes we don't have a data structure to tell us what choices we have. (If we do have an actual tree data structure, backtracking on it is called *depth-first tree searching.*)

3.1 THE BACKTRACKING ALGORITHM

Here is the algorithm (in pseudocode) for doing backtracking, starting from a given node n:

```
function solvable(n):
    if n is a leaf node:
        if n is a goal node, return true
        else return false
    else:
        for each child c of n:
            if solvable(c), return true
        return false
```

Notice that the algorithm is expressed as a boolean function. This is essential to understanding the algorithm. If solvable(n) is true, that means node n is part of a solution—that is, node n is one of the nodes on a path from the root to some goal node. We say that n is **solvable**. If solvable(n) is false, then there is *no* path that includes n to any goal node.

How does this work?

- If any child of n is solvable, then n is solvable.

- If no child of n is solvable, then n is not solvable.

Hence, to decide whether any non-leaf node n is solvable (part of a path to a goal node), all you have to do is test whether any child of n is solvable. This is done recursively, on each child of n. In the above code, this is done by the lines

```
for each child c of n:
    if solvable(c), return true
return false
```

Eventually, the recursion will "bottom out" at a leaf node. If the leaf node is a goal node, it is solvable; if the leaf node is not a goal node, it is not solvable. This is our base case. In the above code, this is done by the lines

```
if n is a leaf node:
    if n is a goal node, return true
    else return false
```

The backtracking algorithm is simple and important. You should understand it thoroughly. Another way of stating it is as follows:

To search a tree:

1. If the tree consists of a single leaf, test whether it is a goal node, and return the result;

2. Otherwise, search the subtrees of this tree until you find one containing a goal node, or until you have searched them all without finding a goal node.

In the above, we have assumed that any goal node would be a leaf. The algorithm can easily be adapted to the case where goal nodes may occur within the tree, not just at the leaves.

3.2 NONRECURSIVE BACKTRACKING

Backtracking is a rather typical recursive algorithm, and any recursive algorithm can be rewritten as a stack algorithm. In fact, that is how your recursive algorithms are translated into machine or assembly language.

```
boolean solve(Node n):
    put node n on the stack
    while the stack is not empty:
        topnode = the node at the top of the stack
        if topnode is a leaf:
            if it is a goal node, return true
            else pop it off the stack
        else:
            if topnode has untried children:
                push the next untried child onto the stack
```

```
        else pop the node off the stack
    return false
```

Starting from the root, the only nodes that can be pushed onto the stack are the children of the node currently on the top of the stack, and these are only pushed on one child at a time; hence, the nodes on the stack always describe a valid path in the tree. Nodes are removed from the stack only when it is known that they have no goal nodes among their descendants. Therefore, if the root node gets removed (making the stack empty), there must have been no goal nodes at all, and no solution to the problem.

When the stack algorithm terminates successfully, the nodes on the stack form (in reverse order) a path from the root to a goal node.

Similarly, when the recursive algorithm finds a goal node, the path information is embodied (in reverse order) in the sequence of recursive calls. Thus as the recursion unwinds, the path can be recovered one node at a time, by (for instance) printing the node at the current level, or storing it in an array.

Here is the recursive backtracking algorithm, modified slightly to print (in reverse order) the nodes along the successful path:

```
boolean solve(Node n) {
    if n is a leaf node {
        if the leaf is a goal node {
            print n
            return true
        }
        else return false
    } else {
        for each child c of n {
            if solve(c) succeeds {
                print n
```

```
                return true
            }
        }
        return false
    }
}
```

3.3 KEEPING BACKTRACKING SIMPLE

All of these versions of the backtracking algorithm are pretty simple, but when applied to a real problem, they can get pretty cluttered up with details. Even determining whether the node is a leaf can be complex: for example, if the path represents a series of moves in a chess endgame problem, the leaves are the checkmate and stalemate solutions.

To keep the program clean, therefore, tests like this should be encapsulated in methods. In a chess game, for example, you could test whether a node is a leaf by writing a gameOver method (or you could even call it isLeaf). This method would encapsulate all the ugly details of figuring out whether any possible moves remain.

Notice that the backtracking algorithms require us to keep track, for each node on the current path, which of its children have been tried already (so we don't have to try them again). In the above code, we made this look simple, by just saying for each child c of n. In reality, it may be difficult to figure out what the possible children are, and there may be no obvious way to step through them. In chess, for example, a node can represent one arrangement of pieces on a chessboard, and each child of that node can represent the arrangement after some piece has made a legal move. How do you find these children, and how do you keep track of which ones you've already examined?

The most straightforward way to keep track of which children of the node have been tried is as follows: Upon initial entry to the node (that is, when you first get there from above), make a list of all its children. As you try each child, take it off the list. When the list is empty, there are no remaining untried children, and you can return "failure." This is a simple approach, but it may require quite a lot of additional work.

There is an easier way to keep track of which children have been tried, if you can define an ordering on the children. If there is an ordering, and you know which child you just tried, you can determine which child to try next.

For example, you might be able to number the children 1 through n, and try them in numerical order. Then, if you have just tried child k, you know that you have already tried children 1 through k - 1, and you have not yet tried children k + 1 through n. Or, if you are trying to color a map with just four colors, you can always try red first, then yellow, then green, then blue. If child yellow fails, you know to try child green next. If you are searching a maze, you can try choices in the order left, straight, and right (or perhaps north, east, south, west).

It isn't always easy to find a simple way to order the children of a node. In the chess game example, you might number your pieces (or perhaps the squares of the board) and try them in numerical order; but in addition, each piece may also have several moves, and these must also be ordered.

You can probably find some way to order the children of a node. If the ordering scheme is simple enough, you should use it; but if it is too cumbersome, you are better off keeping a list of untried children.

3.4 PRUNING AND FOUR COLORING

One of the things that simplifies a binary tree search is that, at each choice point, you can ignore all the previous choices.

Previous choices don't give you any information about what you should do next; as far as you know, both the left and the right child are equally likely to be solutions. In many problems, however, you may be able to eliminate children immediately, without recursion. This is called *pruning*.

Consider, for example, the problem of *four-coloring* a map. It is a theorem of mathematics that any map on a plane, no matter how convoluted the countries are (so long as they are not in separate, unconnected pieces), can be colored with at most four colors, so that no two countries that share a border are the same color.

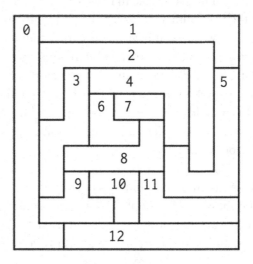

FIGURE 3.2 A map to color with four colors.

Here is one way that we can represent the map shown in Figure 3.2 in Java:

```java
void createMap() {
    map = new int[13][];
    map[0] = new int[] { 1, 2, 3, 9, 12 };
    map[1] = new int[] { 0, 2, 5 };
```

```
    map[2] = new int[] { 0, 1, 3, 4, 5 };
    map[3] = new int[] { 0, 2, 4, 6, 8, 9  };
    map[4] = new int[] { 2, 3, 5, 6, 7, 8 };
    map[5] = new int[] { 1, 2, 4, 8, 11 };
    map[6] = new int[] { 3, 4, 7, 8 };
    map[7] = new int[] { 4, 6, 8 };
    map[8] = new int[] { 3, 4, 5, 6, 7, 9, 10, 11 };
    map[9] = new int[] { 0, 3, 8, 10, 12 };
    map[10] = new int[] { 8, 9, 11, 12 };
    map[11] = new int[] { 5, 8, 10, 12};
    map[12] = new int[] { 0, 9, 10, 11 };
}
```

This problem can be viewed as a *decision tree*. Starting with a completely uncolored map (the root of the decision tree), we have a choice of four different colors for the root node. Having picked a color for the root node, we now have a choice of four colors for the next node (one of its children). And so on.

To color a map, first choose a color for the first country, then a color for the second country, and so on, until all countries are colored. Here are two ways to do this:

Method 1. For each country, recur with each possible color, and continue until there are no more countries. When all countries have been colored, check whether we are at a goal node (the map is correctly colored), and if not, backtrack.

Method 2. For each country, try only those colors that have not already been used for an adjacent country, and recur. Backtrack if no color can be used. If and when we run out of countries, we have successfully colored the map.

In this section, we use Java to describe a backtracking algorithm that solves the map coloring problem. The complete code for

Java can be found in Appendix I, and the equivalent code for Python in Appendix J.

The colors are represented by integers, from RED=1 to BLUE=4, while 0 indicates that a country has not yet been colored. We define the following helper methods. The helper method code isn't displayed here because it's not important for understanding how the backtracking works.

- boolean goodColoring()

  - Used by method 1 to test (at a leaf node) whether the entire map is colored correctly.

- boolean okToColor(int country, int color)

  - Used by method 2 to check, at every node, whether there is an adjacent node already colored with the given color.

Method 1 does not do any pruning, but tries each possible coloring until it finds one that works:

```java
boolean explore1(int country, Color color) {
    if (country >= map.length)
        return goodColoring();
    mapColors[country] = color;
    for (Color c : Color.values()) {
        if (explore1(country + 1, c)) {
            return true;
        }
    }
    mapColors[country] = Color.NONE;
    return false;
}
```

Method 2 prunes by eliminating a color for a country if some adjacent country already has that color:

```
boolean explore2(int country, Color color) {
    if (country >= map.length)
        return true;
    if (okToColor(country, color)) {
        mapColors[country] = color;
        for (Color i : Color.values()) {
            if (explore2(country + 1, i))
                return true;
        }
    }
    return false;
}
```

The two methods seem pretty similar. You might expect the method that does pruning to be faster, and you would be correct. You might, however, be surprised at just how much faster it is. Here is a typical timing result:

Method 1: 2355638070 ns.

Method 2: 20516 ns.

In other words, method 1 takes about 115 thousand times longer on this particular problem. The difference is that the second method stops searching as soon as it detects that, with the choices made so far, no solution is possible. When coloring a country, if an adjacent country already has that color, it does not explore further.

Because Python is a dynamic language, it is inherently slower than Java. Here are the results of a run in Python:

Method 1: 575.22 seconds (almost 10 minutes)

Method 2: 0.0574 seconds

In this trial, method 1 is almost exactly one hundred thousand times slower, very comparable to the results in Java.

The point is not that Python is slower than Java; today's computers are fast enough that the difference matters only in a few kinds of resource-intensive programs. Rather, the point is that the expense of backtracking is exponential on the size of the problem. To deal with anything other than toy problems, pruning is not a luxury, but a necessity.

3.5 BINARY TREE SEARCH I

For starters, let's do the simplest possible example of backtracking, which is searching an actual tree. We will also use the simplest kind of tree, a binary tree.

> **Reminder:** A *binary tree* is a data structure composed of *nodes*. One node is designated as the *root node*. Each node has a *value*, a *left child*, and a *right child*, where each child could be "empty" (null or None). A node with only empty children is called a *leaf*.

For our purposes, we will say that the value in a node will be its name, and in addition the node will contain a boolean value to tell whether it is a goal node. The first example in this chapter (which we repeat here) shows a binary tree (Figure 3.3).

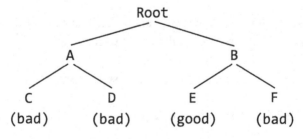

FIGURE 3.3   A tree with one good leaf.

Here's a definition of a `BinaryTree` class in Java (slightly modified from the version given earlier):

```java
public class BinaryTree {
    String name;
    BinaryTree leftChild = null;
    BinaryTree rightChild = null;
    boolean isGoalNode = false;

    BinaryTree(String name,
               BinaryTree left,
               BinaryTree right,
               boolean isGoalNode) {
        this.name = name;
        leftChild = left;
        rightChild = right;
        this.isGoalNode = isGoalNode;
    }
}
```

As defined above, the "value" in each node is its name, of type `String`. To make a more special-purpose binary tree, this class should be genericized, so that the binary tree could contain values of any type. Our goal here, however, is to keep things simple, and that means ignoring generics.

Another unusual thing about the above code is that every node in a binary tree is marked as to whether it is a goal node. In an actual program, this would involve computation (Are there three Xs in a row? Is the opponent's king in check?). Again, the goal is simplicity.

Here's the equivalent code in Python.

```python
class BinaryTree(object):

    def __init__(self, name, left_child,
                 right_child, is_goal_node):
```

```
self.name = name
self.left_child = left_child
self.right_child = right_child
self.is_goal_node = is_goal_node
```

Next we will create a TreeSearch class, and in it we will define a method makeTree() which constructs the above binary tree. In Java:

```
static BinaryTree makeTree() {
    BinaryTree root, a, b, c, d, e, f;
    c = new BinaryTree("C", null, null, false);
    d = new BinaryTree("D", null, null, false);
    e = new BinaryTree("E", null, null, true);
    f = new BinaryTree("F", null, null, false);
    a = new BinaryTree("A", c, d, false);
    b = new BinaryTree("B", e, f, false);
    root = new BinaryTree("Root", a, b, false);
    return root;
}
```

And in Python:

```
def make_tree():
    c = BinaryTree('C', None, None, False)
    d = BinaryTree('D', None, None, False)
    e = BinaryTree('E', None, None, True)
    f = BinaryTree('F', None, None, False)
    a = BinaryTree('A', c, d, False)
    b = BinaryTree('B', e, f, False)
    root = BinaryTree('Root', a, b, False)
    return root
```

Notice the order in which the tree nodes were constructed. Our constructor requires values for the left subtree and the right subtree, so either we have to construct those first, or we have to go back later and fill them in. In other words, we have to work from the leaves up to the root.

Here's a main method in Java to create a binary tree and try to solve it:

```java
public static void main(String args[]) {
    BinaryTree tree = makeTree();
    System.out.println(solvable(tree));
}
```

And Python:

```python
def main():
    tree = make_tree()
    print(solvable(tree))
```

And finally, here is the recursive backtracking routine (in pseudocode) to "solve" the binary tree by finding a goal node. This code only determines whether there is a goal node; it does not report how to get to it from the root.

```
function solvable(binaryTree):
    1. if node is null/None, return false
    2. if node is a goal node return true
    3. if solvable(node.leftChild), return true
    4. if solvable(node.rightChild), return true
    5. return false
}
```

Here's what the numbered lines are doing:

1. A null node is not solvable. This statement is so that we can call this method with the children of a node, without first checking whether those children actually exist.

2. If the node we are given is a goal node, return success.

3. See if the left child of node is solvable, and if so, conclude that node is solvable. We will only get to this line if node is non-null and is not a goal node.

4. See if the right child of node is solvable, and if so, conclude that node is solvable. We will only get to this line if node is neither null nor a goal node, and if the left child of node is not solvable.

5. If we get here, neither child of node is solvable, so node itself is not solvable.

This program runs correctly and, when used with the above example tree, returns true as the result.

3.6 BINARY TREE SEARCH II

There is a problem with the code that we have developed so far. Our solvable method returns a *boolean* result: true if there is a solution, false if there is not. We might want to know more than that. We might want to know how to get to a solution; that is, what path do we follow to get to a goal state?

If we are doing things recursively, the solution is to accumulate the results in a list. When a goal node is found, create a list and put that node in it. Then, as the recursion "unwinds," put each node in turn into the list.

Java has lists, of course, but they are complex and use non-standard terminology. For our purposes we will instead use the List class defined in Section 2.2.1. Python's lists are much simpler, so we will use those directly.

Again, we use strings as the values in the list (the head), and this could be generalized. For simplicity, head and tail are publicly available variables, not methods.

Now, instead of a solvable method that only returns true or false, we can write a solve method that returns a path from the root node to the goal. Here it is in Java:

```
/**
 * Find goal node and report path.
 */
static List solve(BinaryTree node) {
    List temp;
    if (node == null) {
        return null;
    }
    if (node.isGoalNode) {
        return new List(node.name, null);
    }
    temp = solve(node.leftChild);
    if (temp != null) {
        return new List(node.name, temp);
    }
    temp = solve(node.rightChild);
    if (temp != null) {
        return new List(node.name, temp);
    }
    return null;
}
```

And in Python:

```python
def solve(node):
    """Find goal node and report path."""
    if node == None:
        return None

    if node.is_goal_node:
        return [node.name]

    temp = solve(node.left_child)
    if temp != None:
        return [node.name] + temp

    temp = solve(node.right_child)
```

```
        if temp != None:
            return [node.name] + temp

    return None
```

Now, if we call solve with the BinaryTree that we have been using as an example, it produces a list as a result. If we print the list, we get … well, Python prints something useful, but in Java, we get something like List@6d06d69c. If we want to actually see the results, we need to add a toString method to our List class. We might as well do that recursively.

We begin with some pseudocode:

```
function toString(list):
    if the tail is null, return the head
    else return head + toString(the tail)
```

This recursive method takes a list as a parameter. Unfortunately, the toString method, in order to properly override the version inherited from Object, cannot have parameters. For this reason, we move the recursion into a helper method, contents, and have toString call contents.

```
@Override
public String toString() {
    String s = ("[ ");
    s += contents(this);
    return s + ("]");
}

private String contents(List list) {
    if (list.tail == null) {
        return list.head + " ";
    } else {
        return list.head + " " + contents(list.tail);
    }
}
```

With this addition, the resultant list prints as [Root B E].

If the above code looks familiar, it is because we have previously written the equivalent function in Python.

Complete code for binary tree searching is given in Appendix C for Java and in Appendix D for Python.

3.7 TREE AND GRAPH SEARCHES

A node in a binary tree may have a left child, a right child, or neither or both of these. A node in a (general) tree, on the other hand, may have any number of children.

To search a (finite) binary tree for a goal node, the algorithm is really quite simple.

```
To search from a node:
    if the node doesn't exist, return false.
    if the node is a goal node, return success.
    if searching from the left child succeeds,
        return success.
    if searching from the right child succeeds,
        return success.
    return failure.
```

The algorithm for searching a general tree is practically the same,

```
To search from a node:
    if the node is a goal node,
        return success.
    for each child of the node:
        if searching from that child succeeds,
            return success.
    return failure.
```

Binary trees and general trees do not contain cycles. That is, by going "down" into a tree, following links to children, you will never find yourself back at the same node you started from.

Graphs may contain cycles. By going from one node to the next, you might find yourself back where you started. Graphs are not hierarchically organized and do not have one distinguished root node, so instead of referring to the children of a node, we talk about its *neighbors*—the other nodes you can get to from this node.

Searching a graph is like searching a tree, except that we want to avoid getting stuck in a cycle, visiting the same nodes over and over again. In principle, this is simple—any time we visit a node we've been to before, call that a failure. After all, we didn't find anything the last time we were here, so we won't this time, either.

```
To search from a node:
    if the node is a goal node,
        return success.
    if we've been at this node before,
        return failure.
    for each neighbor of the node:
        if searching from that neighbor succeeds,
            return success.
    return failure.
```

There are two basic ways to tell if we've been at a node before.

1. When we get to the node, look for a mark. If there is one, we know we've been there before, so we don't need to search from there again. Otherwise, mark it and continue the search.

   - A *marking algorithm* both looks at values in the graph and changes them. This is contrary to our general advice not to do both in a recursion. However, in this case, we don't have to consider other levels of the recursion—either we've been to this node before, or we haven't.

2. Keep a set of all the nodes we've been to, and look to see if this node is in that set. If not, add it to the set.

As an example, suppose you want to get from Smallville to Metropolis. You have a map on which the cities are nodes, and two cities are neighbors if there is a highway from one to the other, with no intervening cities. A simple graph search will (eventually) find a path from one to the other.

This example suggests a number of ways in which the search might be improved. We might have distances marked on each highway between two cities, and we would prefer to minimize distances. We might know that Metropolis is east of Smallville, so we would prefer to go in that direction. Some roads might be toll roads, which we can take if there isn't a better alternative. Some roads might be one-way. And so on.

Most libraries provide list, binary tree, and tree objects, but not graph objects. Because of the high variability in types and uses of graphs, there is not a "best" way to represent a graph, nor is there a best way to search a graph. Implementation of graph structures is usually left up to the individual programmer.

3.8 DEBUGGING TECHNIQUES

Often our first try at a program doesn't work, and we need to debug it.

We have emphasized that one should not "look down" into a recursion when trying to write or understand a recursive routine. Debuggers are sometimes helpful, but using one to debug a recursive routine strongly encourages just this approach, because you can only see the state of the program from moment to moment. Using print statements can be much more helpful for this kind of debugging; they allow you to see the overall structure, and to match calls with results.

There are some simple tricks to making effective use of print statements. These tricks can be applied to any program, but are especially useful when you are trying to debug recursive routines.

Trick #1: Indent when you print method entries and exits. Often, the best debugging technique is to print every method call and return (or at least the most important ones). You probably want to print, for each method, what parameters it came in with, and what value it leaves with. However, if you just print a long list of these, it's hard to match up method exits with their corresponding entries. Indentation that shows the level of nesting can help.

Indenting requires keeping track of the current level of indentation. This can be done with an additional parameter, or with the use of a global variable. The use of global variables is strongly discouraged in general, but if a global variable is used only for this one purpose, it should not affect the proper functioning of the code.

Trick #2: Use specialized print methods for debugging. Don't clutter up your actual code more than you must. Also, remember that code inserted for debugging purposes can itself contain bugs, or (in the worst case) can affect the results, so be very careful with it.

When debugging, it is useful to see what arguments each function is called with, and what value it returns. This is some of the same information provided by a debugger, but printed, so it can be seen all at once. For tracing the binary tree search, we will use the following methods:

- `void enter(BinaryTree node)`—Prints the name of the function being entered and the value of its parameter, then increases the indentation level. A call to this method will be the first line of each function we want to trace.

- `boolean yes()`—Reduces the indentation level, prints an exit message, and returns `true`. We will replace each `return true` with `return yes()`.

- boolean no()—Reduces the indentation level, prints an exit message, and returns false. We will replace each return false with return no().

- String name(BinaryTree node)—A helper method to return the name of the node, or null if given a null node.

As written, these debugging methods are specific to the tree search problem; more general versions are given in Appendix E for Java and Appendix F for Python.

Here is an implementation of the methods in Java.

```java
static String indent = "";

static String name(BinaryTree node) {
    if (node == null) return null;
    else return node.name;
}

static void enter(BinaryTree node) {
    System.out.println(indent + "Entering solvable(" +
                       name(node) + ")");
    indent = indent + "|  ";
}

static boolean yes(BinaryTree node) {
    indent = indent.substring(3);
    System.out.println(indent + "solvable(" +
                       name(node) + ") returns true");
    return true;
}

static boolean no(BinaryTree node) {
    indent = indent.substring(3);
    System.out.println(indent + "solvable(" +
                       name(node) + ") returns false");
    return false;
}
```

To use this code, we modify solvable. Here is the original version:

```
static boolean solvable(BinaryTree node) {
    if (node == null) return false;
    if (node.isGoalNode) return true;
    if (solvable(node.leftChild)) return true;
    if (solvable(node.rightChild)) return true;
    return false;
}
```

Here is the modified version:

```
static boolean solvable(BinaryTree node) {
    enter(node);
    if (node == null) return no(node);
    if (node.isGoalNode) return yes(node);
    if (solvable(node.leftChild)) return yes(node);
    if (solvable(node.rightChild)) return yes(node);
    return no(node);
}
```

And here is the result:

```
Entering solvable(Root)
|  Entering solvable(A)
|  |  Entering solvable(C)
|  |  |  Entering solvable(null)
|  |  |  solvable(null) returns false
|  |  |  Entering solvable(null)
|  |  |  solvable(null) returns false
|  |  solvable(C) returns false
|  |  Entering solvable(D)
|  |  |  Entering solvable(null)
|  |  |  solvable(null) returns false
|  |  |  Entering solvable(null)
|  |  |  solvable(null) returns false
|  |  solvable(D) returns false
|  solvable(A) returns false
```

```
|  Entering solvable(B)
|  |  Entering solvable(E)
|  |  solvable(E) returns true
|  solvable(B) returns true
solvable(Root) returns true
```

Trick #3: Never discard your debugging statements. Writing debugging statements is programming, too. Often it's as much work to debug the debugging statements as it is to debug the actual program. Once your program is working, why throw this code away?

Obviously, you don't want to print out all this debugging information from a program you are ready to submit (or to turn over to your manager). You could comment out the debugging calls, but that can be a lot of work. What's more, in the above example, you would have to replace every return yes(node) with return true, and every return no(node) with return false. All these changes might introduce new bugs into your program.

The simple solution is to make your debugging statements conditional. For example,

```
static final boolean debugging = false;

static void enter(BinaryTree node) {
    if (debugging) {
        System.out.println(indent +
            "Entering solvable(" +
                            name(node) +
                            ")");
        indent = indent + "|  ";
    }
}

static boolean yes(BinaryTree node) {
    if (debugging) {
```

```
            indent = indent.substring(3);
            System.out.println(indent +
                            "solvable(" +
                            name(node) +
                            ") returns true");
        }
        return true;
    }

    static boolean no(BinaryTree node) {
        if (debugging) {
            indent = indent.substring(3);
            System.out.println(indent +
                            "solvable(" +
                            name(node) +
                            ") returns false");
        }
        return false;
    }
```

In industry, actual programs often have multiple flags to control different aspects of debugging. Don't worry too much about making your code larger; modern compilers will notice that since the variable debugging is final, it can never be true, and the debugging code will be discarded.

Trick #4: To find out how you got to a particular place in the code, create an Exception and print its stack trace.

Since an Exception is an object like any other, you can create and throw your own exceptions. However, Java programmers don't always realize that you can create an Exception without throwing it. Instead, you can simply use it to print out a stack trace. For example, the following code

```
new Exception("Alpha").printStackTrace(System.out);
```

will print out a message something like this, and the program will then continue normally. That is, the above code just acts like a print statement.

```
java.lang.Exception: Alpha
    at TreeSearch.solvable(TreeSearch.java:53)
    at TreeSearch.solvable(TreeSearch.java:57)
    at TreeSearch.main(TreeSearch.java:72)
    etc.
```

A similar trick works in Python.

```
import traceback
traceback.print_stack()
```

3.9 THE FROG PUZZLE

The following puzzle is sometimes called the "frog puzzle." You have some number n of frogs facing right and the same number of toads facing left. The playing board consists simply of a line of 2n + 1 spaces on which to put the frogs and toads. Start with the right-facing frogs on the left end, the left-facing toads at the right end, and a single free space in between. The goal is to reverse the positions of the frogs and toads (Figure 3.4A and 3.4B)

FIGURE 3.4A   Starting position of the frog puzzle.

FIGURE 3.4B   Desired final position.

The frogs and toads can only move forward; they cannot back up. At each move, a frog or toad can either

- move one space ahead, if that space is clear, or
- jump ahead over exactly one frog or toad, if the space just beyond that frog or toad is clear.

For example, you could make the sequence of moves shown in Figures 3.4C–3.4H.

FIGURE 3.4C   Starting position of the frog puzzle.

FIGURE 3.4D   Frog has moved ahead.

FIGURE 3.4E   Toad has jumped frog.

FIGURE 3.4F   Frog has moved ahead.

FIGURE 3.4G   Frog has jumped toad.

FIGURE 3.4H Toad has moved ahead; no more moves are possible.

Now to the program. The main program will initialize the board, and call a recursive backtracking routine to attempt to solve the puzzle. The backtracking routine will either succeed and print out a winning path, or it will fail, and the main program will have to print out the bad news.

The backtracking method below is named solveAndPrint. It has no way to return a solution; rather, it just prints its results as it returns from finding a goal state. The method has to check whether it is at a leaf, which in this case means a position from which no further moves are possible.

Each possible move will result in a new board position, and these new board positions are the *children* of the current board position. Hence to find the children of a node (that is, of a board position), we need only find the possible moves from that node. Remember that it is also highly desirable to find an order on these possible moves.

Here, it is time to stop and take thought. To make progress, we must analyze the game to some extent. Probably a number of approaches would work, and what follows is based on the way I worked it out. If you were to program this puzzle, you might find a different but equally valid approach.

First, notice that if a frog or toad has a move, that move is unique: if it can move ahead one square, then it cannot jump. If it can jump, it cannot move ahead one square. This suggests that to find the possible moves, we might assign numbers to the frogs and toads, and check each one in turn. When we have looked at all the frogs and toads, we have looked at all the possible moves. This would require having a table to keep track of where each frog or toad is, or else somehow "marking" each one with its number and searching the board each time to find the one we want. Neither alternative is very attractive.

Next, notice that for a given board position, each frog or toad occupies a unique space. Hence, instead of talking about moving a particular frog or toad, we can talk about moving the frog or toad in a particular space. If a move is possible from a given space, then that must be the only move possible from that space, because if the frog or toad in that space has a move, it is unique. There is a slight complication because not every space contains a frog or toad, but at least the spaces (unlike the frogs and toads) stay in one place.

Now we have a simpler ordering of moves to use in our program. Just check, in order, the $2n + 1$ spaces of the board. For each space, either there is exactly one move, or no move is possible. With this understanding, we can write a canMove method to determine whether a move is possible from a given position:

- If the position is empty, no move is possible;

- If the position contains a right-facing frog, the method checks for a move or jump to the right;

- If the position contains a left-facing toad, the method checks for a move or jump to the left.

We write another method makeMove that will take a board and a position, make a move from that position, and return as its value a new board. (We could write this somewhat more efficiently by changing the old board, rather than creating a new one, but here we are more concerned with simplicity.)

Here is the central backtracking method in Python:

```python
def solve_and_print(board):
    """Recursively solve the puzzle and print
       the reversed sequence of boards."""
    if puzzle_solved(board):
        return True
    for i in range(0, len(board)):
        if can_move(board, i):
            new_board = make_move(board, i)
            if solve_and_print(new_board):
                print_board(board)
                return True
    return False
```

And in Java:

```java
/**
 * Recursively solve the puzzle and print
 * the reversed sequence of boards.
 */
boolean solveAndPrint(String[] board) {
    if (puzzleSolved(board)) {
        return true;
    }
    for (int position = 0;
            position < BOARD_SIZE;
            position++) {
        if (canMove(board, position)) {
            String[] newBoard =
                makeMove(board, position);
            if (solveAndPrint(newBoard)) {
                printBoard(newBoard);
                return true;
            }
        }
    }
    return false;
}
```

Along with canMove and makeMove, we are using methods puzzleSolved and printBoard with meanings that should be obvious.

Here is some output from the Java version of the program; the output from Python is similar:

```
Toad Toad Toad [  ] Frog Frog Frog
Toad Toad Toad Frog [  ] Frog Frog
Toad Toad [  ] Frog Toad Frog Frog
Toad [  ] Toad Frog Toad Frog Frog
Toad Frog Toad [  ] Toad Frog Frog
Toad Frog Toad Frog Toad [  ] Frog
Toad Frog Toad Frog Toad Frog [  ]
Toad Frog Toad Frog [  ] Frog Toad
Toad Frog [  ] Frog Toad Frog Toad
[  ] Frog Toad Frog Toad Frog Toad
Frog [  ] Toad Frog Toad Frog Toad
Frog Frog Toad [  ] Toad Frog Toad
Frog Frog Toad Frog Toad [  ] Toad
Frog Frog Toad Frog [  ] Toad Toad
Frog Frog [  ] Frog Toad Toad Toad
Frog Frog Frog [  ] Toad Toad Toad
```

Notice that the solution is given in reverse order: Frogs start out on the left and toads on the right, as in the last line. This is because once a solution is found, it is printed out from the recursive routine as that routine unwinds. To return a solution, rather than just print it out, the steps should be saved in a stack, and the stack returned to the calling program.

Complete programs for the frog puzzle are given in Appendix G for Java and Appendix H for Python.

3.10 FROGS ACCUMULATOR

In the previous section, we implemented the Frog Puzzle, using a rather awkward solveAndPrint method. As the name implied, the method was not able to return a solution to the caller; it could only print the solution (in reverse order). Mixing I/O and computation together in a single function is poor style. Using a façade method and an accumulator, we can now write a purely computational solve method.

```
List solve(String[] board) {
    return new List(board, solve(board, null));
}

private List solve(String[] board, List acc) {
    if (puzzleSolved(board)) {
        return new List(board, acc);
    }
    for (int position = 0;
            position < BOARD_SIZE;
            position++) {
        if (canMove(board, position)) {
            String[] newBoard =
                    makeMove(board, position);
            List result = solve(newBoard, acc);
            if (result != null) {
                return new List(newBoard, result);
            }
        }
    }
    return null;
}
```

We can mirror this logic in Python:

```
def solve(board):
    """Façade method."""
    return [board] + solve2(board, [])

def solve2(board, acc):
    """Recursively solve the frog puzzle."""
    if puzzle_solved(board):
        return [board] + acc
```

```
        for i in range(0, len(board)):
            if can_move(board, i):
                new_board = make_move(board, i)
                result = solve2(new_board, acc)
                if result != []:
                    return [new_board] + result
        return []
```

The above functions are essentially correct, but with a minor problem: The final (solved) board occurs twice at the end of the list. This occurs in part because, in our simple implementation, we cannot distinguish between an empty list and a failure flag; both are represented by null (Java) or None (Python). The problem can be corrected by moving the puzzle_solved test further down into the function.

```
    def solve2(board, acc):
        """Recursively solve the frog puzzle."""
        for i in range(0, len(board)):
            if can_move(board, i):
                new_board = make_move(board, i)
                if puzzle_solved(new_board):
                    return [new_board] + acc
                result = solve2(new_board, acc)
                if result != []:
                    return [new_board] + result
        return []
```

The same change in logic can be applied to the Java version.

With this change, the test for the base case is not the first thing done by the method. That makes the method somewhat harder to understand, but still not terribly difficult.

Afterword

R ecursion is all too often considered to be an "advanced" topic. While this little volume has covered a number of advanced topics that involve recursion—tail recursion, pruning, recursive data structures, the use of accumulators, and backtracking— recursion itself is simple.

As an experiment, I began using some recursive examples in my introductory programming courses, without even mentioning the term "recursion." The course had a laboratory setting where I and my assistants went from student to student, helping them with their problems, so it was easy to tell which concepts caused difficulty. Beginners had all the usual problems, such as getting loop indices correct and deciding when to use functions, but the occasional use of recursion caused no additional problems.

As the saying goes, "When your only tool is a hammer, every problem looks like a nail." Recursion is another tool in your programming toolbox. Sometimes it's the right tool; sometimes it isn't. Throughout this book, I've tried to suggest appropriate uses, but in the end, your own experience will be your best guide.

DOI: 10.1201/9781003359616-4

Appendix A: Quicksort in Java

```java
public static void quicksort(int[] array,
                             int left,
                             int right) {
    if (left < right) {
        int p = partition(array, left, right);
        quicksort(array, left, p - 1);
        quicksort(array, p + 1, right);
    }
}

static int partition(int[] arr, int lo, int hi) {
    int pivot = arr[hi];
    int i = lo - 1;
    for (int j = lo; j < hi; j++) {
        if (arr[j] < pivot) {
            i += 1;
            swap(arr, i, j);
        }
    }
    swap(arr, i + 1, hi);
    return i + 1;
}
```

```java
static void swap(int[] arr, int i, int j) {
    int temp = arr[i];
    arr[i] = arr[j];
    arr[j] = temp;
}
```

Appendix B: Quicksort in Python

```python
def quicksort(array, left, right):
    if left < right:
        p = partition(array, left, right)
        quicksort(array, left, p - 1)
        quicksort(array, p + 1, right)

def partition(arr, lo, hi):
    pivot = arr[hi]
    i = lo - 1
    for j in range(lo, hi):
        if arr[j] < pivot:
            i += 1
            arr[i], arr[j] = arr[j], arr[i]
    arr[i + 1], arr[hi] = arr[hi], arr[i + 1]
    return i + 1
```

Appendix C: Binary Tree Search in Java

```java
public class BinaryTree {
    String name;
    BinaryTree leftChild = null;
    BinaryTree rightChild = null;
    boolean isGoalNode = false;

    BinaryTree(String name,
               BinaryTree left,
               BinaryTree right,
               boolean isGoalNode) {
        this.name = name;
        leftChild = left;
        rightChild = right;
        this.isGoalNode = isGoalNode;
    }
}

public class List {
    public String head;
    public List tail;
```

```java
    public List(String head, List tail) {
        this.head = head;
        this.tail = tail;
    }

    @Override
    public String toString() {
        String s = ("[ ");
        s += contents(this);
        return s + ("]");
    }

    private String contents(List list) {
        if (list.tail == null) {
            return list.head + " ";
        } else {
            return list.head + " " + contents(list.tail);
        }
    }
}

public class TreeSearch {

    static BinaryTree makeTree() {
        BinaryTree root, a, b, c, d, e, f;
        c = new BinaryTree("C", null, null, false);
        d = new BinaryTree("D", null, null, false);
        e = new BinaryTree("E", null, null, true);
        f = new BinaryTree("F", null, null, false);
        a = new BinaryTree("A", c, d, false);
        b = new BinaryTree("B", e, f, false);
        root = new BinaryTree("Root", a, b, false);
        return root;
    }

    static boolean solvable(BinaryTree node) {
        if (node == null) return false;
        if (node.isGoalNode) return true;
        if (solvable(node.leftChild)) return true;
```

```java
        if (solvable(node.rightChild)) return true;
        return false;
    }

    static List solve(BinaryTree node) {
        List temp;
        if (node == null) {
            return null;
        }
        if (node.isGoalNode) {
            return new List(node.name, null);
        }
        temp = solve(node.leftChild);
        if (temp != null) {
            return new List(node.name, temp);
        }
        temp = solve(node.rightChild);
        if (temp != null) {
            return new List(node.name, temp);
        }
        return null;
    }

    public static void main(String args[]) {
        BinaryTree tree = makeTree();
        System.out.println(solvable(tree));
        System.out.println(solve(tree));
    }
}
```

Appendix D: Binary Tree Search in Python

```python
class BinaryTree(object):

    def __init__(self, name, left_child,
                 right_child, is_goal_node):
        self.name = name
        self.left_child = left_child
        self.right_child = right_child
        self.is_goal_node = is_goal_node

def make_tree():
    c = BinaryTree('C', None, None, False)
    d = BinaryTree('D', None, None, False)
    e = BinaryTree('E', None, None, True)
    f = BinaryTree('F', None, None, False)
    a = BinaryTree('A', c, d, False)
    b = BinaryTree('B', e, f, False)
    root = BinaryTree('Root', a, b, False)
    return root
```

```python
def solvable(node):
    if node == None: return False
    if node.is_goal_node: return True
    if solvable(node.left_child): return True
    if solvable(node.right_child): return True
    return False

def solve(node):
    if node == None:
        return None
    if node.is_goal_node:
        return [node.name]
    temp = solve(node.left_child)
    if temp != None:
        return [node.name] + temp
    temp = solve(node.right_child)
    if temp != None:
        return [node.name] + temp
    return None

def main():
    tree = make_tree()
    print(solvable(tree))
    print(solve(tree))
main()
```

Appendix E:
Java Debugging

H ERE IS A MORE GENERAL version of the debugging methods enter, yes, and no that are described in the text. Java varargs are used for the parameters of the method being debugged, and redundant printing has been eliminated. In addition, the global variable debugging has been added to make it easy to turn debugging on and off.

```java
static String indent = "";
static boolean debugging = false;

static void enter(String method, Object … args) {
    if (! debugging) return;
    String[] strs = new String[args.length];
    for (int i = 0; i < args.length; i++) {
        strs[i] = "" + args[i];
    }
    String s = indent + method + "(";
    s += String.join(", ", strs) + ")";
    System.out.println(s);
    indent = indent + "|  ";
}
```

```java
static boolean yes() {
    if (! debugging) return true;
    indent = indent.substring(3);
    System.out.println(indent + "true");
    return true;
}

static boolean no() {
    if (! debugging) return false;
    indent = indent.substring(3);
    System.out.println(indent + "false");
    return false;
}
```

For methods that return an object of some kind, rather than a boolean, it is tempting to write something like

```java
static Object result(Object obj) {
    if (! debugging) return obj;
    indent = indent.substring(3);
    System.out.println(indent + obj);
    return obj;
}
```

Unfortunately, while this method can accept any kind of object (or primitive) as an argument, it will return a value of type Object, and this is likely to be unacceptable to the calling program. One solution is to write multiple methods, each with a different type of parameter, for example,

```java
static BinaryTree result(BinaryTree obj) {
    if (! debugging) return obj;
    indent = indent.substring(3);
    System.out.println(indent + obj);
    return obj;
}

static String result(String obj) {
    if (! debugging) return obj;
```

```
    indent = indent.substring(3);
    System.out.println(indent + obj);
    return obj;
}
```

and so on. Alternatively, the debugging methods could be put in a class of their own (probably a good idea) and could be genericized (probably much less helpful).

Appendix F:
Python Debugging

T HE DEBUGGING TECHNIQUE described in the text can also be employed in Python. Two global variables are used: indent, to control the indentation level; and debugging, to turn debugging on or off.

- Put enter(*args*) at the entrance to any method you want to trace. Any number of arguments may be supplied.

- Replace every return True with return yes().

- Replace every return False with return no().

- Replace every return or return None with return nothing().

- Replace every return *value* with return result(*value*).

This can result in a large number of changes in the code, but using the debugging variable means that these changes do not have to be reversed. For example, the solve method in the tree search example changes from:

```python
def solve(node):
    """Find goal node and report path."""
    if node == None:
        return None

    if node.is_goal_node:
        return [node.name]

    temp = solve(node.left_child)
    if temp != None:
        return [node.name] + temp

    temp = solve(node.right_child)
    if temp != None:
        return [node.name] + temp

    return None
```

To:

```python
def solve(node):
    """Find goal node and report path."""
    enter(node)
    if node == None:
        return nothing()

    if node.is_goal_node:
        return result([node.name])

    temp = solve(node.left_child)
    if temp != None:
        return result([node.name] + temp)

    temp = solve(node.right_child)
    if temp != None:
        return result([node.name] + temp)

    return nothing()
```

The tracing methods used are displayed below. All but enter have essentially the same structure. In fact, only enter and result are needed; the others are mere convenience functions.

```python
indent = ""
debugging = True

def enter(*args):
    if not debugging: return
    import inspect
    global indent
    fargs = [str(x) for x in args]
    print(indent + inspect.stack()[1].function +
    str(fargs))
    indent += "|  "

def yes():
    if not debugging: return True
    global indent
    indent = indent[3:]
    print(indent + "True")
    return True

def no():
    if not debugging: return False
    global indent
    indent = indent[3:]
    print(indent + "False")
    return False

def result(value):
    if not debugging: return value
    global indent
    indent = indent[3:]
    print(indent + str(value))
    return value

def nothing():
    if not debugging: return None
```

```
global indent
indent = indent[3:]
print(indent + "None") # can be omitted
return None
```

The call inspect.stack()[1].function in the above code may be unfamiliar. It returns the name of the calling method, so that this does not have to be supplied as a parameter.

Appendix G: Frog Puzzle in Java

```java
import java.util.Arrays;

public class FrogPuzzle {
    static final int BOARD_SIZE = 7;
    static String frog = "Frog";
    static String toad = "Toad";
    static String empty = "[  ]";

    public static void main(String[] args) {
        FrogPuzzle bt = new FrogPuzzle();
        String[] board = new String[BOARD_SIZE];
        setup(board);
        bt.solveAndPrint(board);
        bt.printBoard(board);
    }

    /**
     * Create initial board.
     */
    private static void setup(String[] board) {
        int length = board.length;
        int half = length / 2;
        for (int i = 0; i < half; i++) {
```

```
        board[i] = frog;
        board[length - 1 - i] = toad;
    }
    board[half] = empty;
}


    /**
 * Initial solution method: Recursively solve
 * the puzzle and print the reversed sequence
 * of boards.
 */
boolean solveAndPrint(String[] board) {
    if (puzzleSolved(board)) {
        return true;
    }
    for (int position = 0;
            position < BOARD_SIZE;
            position++) {
        if (canMove(board, position)) {
            String[] newBoard =
                makeMove(board, position);
            if (solveAndPrint(newBoard)) {
                printBoard(newBoard);
                return true;
            }
        }
    }
    return false;
}

/**
 * Façade method for revised solution.
 */
List solve(String[] board) {
    return new List(board, solve(board, null));
}

/**
 * Improved solution method: Recursively solve
```

```java
 * the frog puzzle and return the solution.
 */
private List solve(String[] board, List acc) {
    for (int position = 0;
            position < BOARD_SIZE;
            position++) {
        if (canMove(board, position)) {
            String[] newBoard =
                    makeMove(board, position);
            if (puzzleSolved(newBoard)) {
                return new List(newBoard, acc);
            }
            List result = solve(newBoard, acc);
            if (result != null) {
                return new List(newBoard, result);
            }
        }
    }
    return null;
}

/**
 * Print the frog puzzle board.
 */
private void printBoard(String[] board) {
    for (String a : board) {
        System.out.print(a + " ");
    }
    System.out.println();
}

/**
 * Move the frog or toad at board[index],
 * returning a new board, not the original.
 */
private String[] makeMove(String[] board,
                            int index) {
    int next = -1;
    if (board[index] == frog) {
```

```java
        if (isEmpty(board, index + 1)) {
            next = index + 1;
        }
        else next = index + 2;
    }
    else {
        if (isEmpty(board, index - 1)) {
            next = index - 1;
        }
        else next = index - 2;
    }
    String[] nextBoard =
            Arrays.copyOf(board, board.length);
    nextBoard[next] = board[index];
    nextBoard[index] = empty;
    return nextBoard;
}


/**
 * Is move possible from board[index]?
 */
private boolean canMove(String[] board,
                        int index) {
    if (board[index] == frog) {
        return isEmpty(board, index + 1) ||
                isEmpty(board, index + 2);
    }
    if (board[index] == toad) {
        return isEmpty(board, index - 1) ||
                isEmpty(board, index - 2);
    }
    return false;
}


 /**
 * Is board[index] a legal location and empty?
 */
private boolean isEmpty(String[] board,
                        int index) {
```

```java
        return index >= 0 &&
               index < board.length &&
               board[index] == empty;
    }

    /**
     * Test if the goal has been reached.
     */
    private boolean puzzleSolved(String[] board) {
        int half = board.length / 2;
        for (int i = 0; i < half; i++) {
            if (board[i] != toad) return false;
        }
        if (board[half] == empty) {
            //          printBoard(board);
            return true;
        }
        return false;
    }
}
```

Appendix H: Frog Puzzle in Python

```python
frog = 'frog'
toad = 'toad'
empty = '    '

def setup(size):
    """Create initial puzzle state."""
    board = [empty] * size
    for i in range(0, size // 2):
        board[i] = frog
        board[-i - 1] = toad
    return board

def can_move(board, index):
    """Is move possible from board[index]?"""
    if board[index] == frog:
        return (is_empty(board, index + 1) or
                is_empty(board, index + 2))
    if board[index] == toad:
        return (is_empty(board, index - 1) or
                is_empty(board, index - 2+))
    return False
```

```python
def is_empty(board, index):
    """Is board[index] a legal location and empty?"""
    return (index >= 0 and
            index < len(board) and
            board[index] == empty)

def make_move(board, index):
    """Move the frog or toad at board[index],
        returning a new board, not the original."""
    next_board = board[:]
    if board[index] == frog:
        if board[index + 1] == empty:
            next = index + 1
        else:
            next = index + 2
    else: # toad
        if board[index - 1] == empty:
            next = index - 1
        else:
            next = index - 2
    next_board[next] = board[index]
    next_board[index] = empty
    return next_board

def solve_and_print(board):
    """Initial solution method: Recursively
        solve the puzzle and print the reversed
        sequence of boards."""
    if puzzle_solved(board):
        return True
    for i in range(0, len(board)):
        if can_move(board, i):
            new_board = make_move(board, i)
            if solve_and_print(new_board):
                print_board(board)
                return True
    return False
```

```python
def solve(board):
    """Façade method for revised solution."""
    return [board] + solve2(board, [])

def solve2(board, acc):
    """Improved solution method: Recursively
        solve the frog puzzle."""
    for i in range(0, len(board)):
        if can_move(board, i):
            new_board = make_move(board, i)
            if puzzle_solved(new_board):
                return [new_board] + acc
            result = solve2(new_board, acc)
            if result != []:
                return [new_board] + result
    return []

def print_board(board):
    """Print the frog puzzle board."""
    print('-' * (7 * len(board) + 1))
    print('|', ' | '.join(board), '|')
    print('-' * (7 * len(board) + 1))

def puzzle_solved(board):
    """Test if the goal has been reached."""
    half = len(board) // 2
    for i in range(0, half):
        if board[i] != toad:
            return False
    if board[half] == empty:
        print_board(board)
        return True
    return False


def main():
    board = setup(7)
    print_board(board)
    solve_and_print(board)

main()
```

Appendix I:
Map Coloring in Java

```java
public class ColoredMap {

    public enum Color {
        RED, YELLOW, GREEN, BLUE, NONE
    }

    Color[] mapColors = new Color[] {
        Color.NONE, Color.NONE,
        Color.NONE, Color.NONE,
        Color.NONE, Color.NONE,
        Color.NONE, Color.NONE,
        Color.NONE, Color.NONE,
        Color.NONE, Color.NONE,
        Color.NONE
    };
    int map[][];
    Debugging db = new Debugging();

    void createMap() {
        map = new int[13][];
        map[0] = new int[] { 1, 2, 3, 9, 12 };
        map[1] = new int[] { 0, 2, 5 };
        map[2] = new int[] { 0, 1, 3, 4, 5 };
```

```java
map[3] = new int[] { 0, 2, 4, 6, 8, 9 };
map[4] = new int[] { 2, 3, 5, 6, 7, 8 };
map[5] = new int[] { 1, 2, 4, 8, 11 };
map[6] = new int[] { 3, 4, 7, 8 };
map[7] = new int[] { 4, 6, 8 };
map[8] = new int[] { 3, 4, 5, 6, 7, 9, 10, 11 };
map[9] = new int[] { 0, 3, 8, 10, 12 };
map[10] = new int[] { 8, 9, 11, 12 };
map[11] = new int[] { 5, 8, 10, 12};
map[12] = new int[] { 0, 9, 10, 11 };
}


/**
 * Tries all possible map colorings
 * until getting a four-colored map.
 */
boolean explore1(int country, Color color) {
    if (country >= map.length)
        return goodColoring();
    mapColors[country] = color;
    for (Color c : Color.values()) {
        if (explore1(country + 1, c)) {
            return true;
        }
    }
    mapColors[country] = Color.NONE;
    return false;
}


/**
 * Uses pruning to find a four-colored map.
 */
boolean explore2(int country, Color color) {
    // Backtracking with pruning
    if (country >= map.length)
        return true;
    if (okToColor(country, color)) {
        mapColors[country] = color;
        for (Color i : Color.values()) {
```

```java
            if (explore2(country + 1, i))
                return true;
        }
    }
    return false;
}

/**
 * Returns true if no country adjacent to this
 * one has already been given this color.
 */
boolean okToColor(int country, Color color) {
    if (color == Color.NONE) return false;
    for (int i = 0; i < map[country].length; i++) {
        int ithAdjCountry = map[country][i];
        if (mapColors[ithAdjCountry] == color) {
            return false;
        }
    }
    return true;
}

/**
 * Return true if the map is properly colored.
 */
boolean goodColoring() {
    for (int i = 0; i < map.length; i++) {
        for (int j = 0; j < map[i].length; j++) {
            if (mapColors[i] ==
            mapColors[map[i][j]]) {
                return false;
            }
        }
    }
    return true;
}

void printMap() {
    for (int i = 0; i < mapColors.length; i++) {
```

```java
            System.out.println("map[" + i + "] is " +
                mapColors[i]);
        }
    }

    public static void main(String args[]) {
        ColoredMap m;
        long ns;

        m = new ColoredMap();
        m.createMap();
        ns = System.nanoTime();
        m.explore1(0, Color.RED);
        ns = System.nanoTime() - ns;
        m.printMap();
        System.out.println(ns + " ns.\n");

        m = new ColoredMap();
        m.createMap();
        ns = System.nanoTime();
        m.explore2(0, Color.RED);
        ns = System.nanoTime() - ns;
        m.printMap();
        System.out.println(ns + " ns.\n");
    }
}
```

Appendix J: Map Coloring in Python

```python
import time

colors = ['RED', 'YELLOW', 'GREEN', 'BLUE', 'NONE']

def create_map():
    global map, map_colors
    map_colors = [None] * 13
    map = [None] * 13
    map[0] = [ 1, 2, 3, 9, 12 ]
    map[1] = [ 0, 2, 5 ]
    map[2] = [ 0, 1, 3, 4, 5 ]
    map[3] = [ 0, 2, 4, 6, 8, 9 ]
    map[4] = [ 2, 3, 5, 6, 7, 8 ]
    map[5] = [ 1, 2, 4, 8, 11 ]
    map[6] = [ 3, 4, 7, 8 ]
    map[7] = [ 4, 6, 8 ]
    map[8] = [ 3, 4, 5, 6, 7, 9, 10, 11 ]
    map[9] = [ 0, 3, 8, 10, 12 ]
    map[10] = [ 8, 9, 11, 12 ]
```

```python
map[11] = [ 5, 8, 10, 12]
map[12] = [ 0, 9, 10, 11 ]

def explore1(country, color):
    """Tries all possible map colorings
        until finding one that works."""
    if country >= len(map):
        return good_coloring();
    map_colors[country] = color
    for c in colors:
        if explore1(country + 1, c):
            return True;
    return False


def explore2(country, color):
    """Uses pruning to ignore map
        colorings that cannot work."""
    if country >= len(map):
        return True
    if ok_to_color(country, color):
        map_colors[country] = color
        for c in colors:
            if explore2(country + 1, c):
                return True
    return False


def ok_to_color(country, color):
    """Returns true if this color is not
        in use by any adjacent country."""
    if color == 'NONE':
        return False
    for i in range(0, len(map[country])):
        ith_adj_country = map[country][i]
        if (map_colors[ith_adj_country] == color):
            return False
    return True


def good_coloring():
    """Returns true if a four-coloring
```

```python
        has been found."""
    for i in range(0, len(map)):
            for j in range(0, len(map[i])):
                if map_colors[i] == map_colors[map[i][j]]:
                    return False
    return True

def main():
    global map_colors

    m = create_map()
    start = time.time()
    explore2(0, 'RED')
    print(map_colors)
    end = time.time()
    print("time: ", end - start)

    m = create_map()
    start = time.time()
    explore1(0, 'RED')
    print(map_colors)
    end = time.time()
    print("time: ", end - start)

main()
```

Appendix K:
Lists in Python

P YTHON'S "LISTS" BEAR LITTLE resemblance to conventional singly linked lists. In most cases, it is easier to treat Python's lists as arrays, and use loops rather than recursion to process them. Recursion should be used for data structures which, unlike Python's lists, are recursively defined.

The following is code for a simple implementation of singly linked lists.

```python
class List:
    def __init__(self, head, tail=None):
        """Construct a List."""
        self.head = head
        self.tail = tail

    def __str__(self):
        """Return a string representation
            of this List."""
        return '[' + self.contents() + ']'

    def contents(self):
        """Return a string representation of
```

```
                the contents of this List."""
        s = str(self.head)
        if self.tail != None:
            s += ' ' + self.tail.contents()
        return s

    def __eq__(self, other):
        """Test if this List equals other."""
        if type(other) != List:
            return False
        if self == []:
            return other == [];
        if other == []:
            return False
        return (self.head == other.head and
                self.tail == other.tail)
```

Within the class, we use the word self to refer to the list being operated on. For methods outside the class, we will use the variable lst. It is inadvisable to spell this as 'list,' because doing so would replace the usual meaning of that word.

```
def to_List(lst):
    """Convert Python list to List."""
    if lst == []:
        return None
    if type(lst[0]) == list:
        head = to_List(lst[0])
    else:
        head = lst[0]
    return List(head, to_List(lst[1:]))

def member(x, lst):
    """Test if x is a top-level element
        of List lst."""
    if lst == None: # out of elements
        return False
    if lst.head == x:
```

```
            return True
        else:
            return member(x, lst.tail)

def deep_member(x, lst):
    """Test if x is a member, at any level,
        of List lst."""
    if lst == None:
        return False
    if lst.head == x:
        return True
    if type(lst.head) == List:
        if deep_member(x, lst.head):
            return True
    return deep_member(x, lst.tail)

def length(lst):
    """Return the number of top-level
        elements in List lst."""
    if lst == None:
        return 0
    return 1 + length(lst.tail)
```

Appendix L:
Trees in Java

T HE FOLLOWING IS A REASONABLY complete implementation of a general Tree class. It includes a parse method for converting a string representation of a Tree into a Tree of Strings.

```java
import java.util.ArrayList;
import java.util.Iterator;
import java.util.LinkedList;
import java.util.List;
import java.util.StringTokenizer;

/**
 * General tree class.
 */
public class Tree<V> {
    public V value;
    private ArrayList<Tree<V>> children;

    /**
     * Constructs a single Tree node with the given value.
     */
    public Tree(V value) {
        this.value = value;
```

```java
        children = new ArrayList<Tree<V>>();
    }


    /**
     * Tests whether the given Object is a Tree
     * that is equal to this Tree.
     */
    @Override
    public boolean equals(Object o) {
        if (!(o instanceof Tree)) {
            return false;
        }
        Tree<?> that = (Tree) o;

        if (! eq(this.value, that.value)) {
            return false;
        }
        return this.children.equals(that.children);
    }


    /**
     * Tests whether two possibly null values are equal.
     */
    private static boolean eq(Object o1, Object o2) {
        if (o1 == null) {
            return o2 == null;
        }
        return o1.equals(o2);
    }


    /**
     * Returns a list of the children of this node.
     * If the node has no children, an empty list
     *  is returned.
     */
    public List<Tree<V>> children() {
        return children;
    }
```

```java
/**
 * Returns the i-th child of this node.
 */
public Tree<V> getChild(int i) {
    return children.get(i);
}


/**
 * Adds a node as the new last child of this tree.
 */
public Tree<V> addChild(Tree<V> newChild)
    throws IllegalArgumentException {
if (newChild.contains(this)) {
    String message = this + " is already in " +
        newChild;
    throw new IllegalArgumentException(message);
}
children.add(newChild);
return this;
}


/**
 * Creates a new node with the given value and
 * adds it as the last child of this Tree node.
 */
public Tree<V> addChild(V val) {
    children.add(new Tree<V>(val));
    return this;
}


/**
 * Returns a string representing this tree.
 * The string does not contain newlines.
 * The general form of the output is:
 * value(child child … child)<.
 */
@Override
public String toString() {
    if (children.size() == 0) {
```

```java
            return value.toString();
        }
        String result = value + "(";
        boolean first = true;
        for (Tree<V> child : children) {
            if (!first)
                result += " ";
            first = false;
            result += child.toString();
        }
        return result + ")";
    }

    /**
     * Prints this tree as an indented structure.
     */
    public void print() {
        print(this, "");
    }

    /**
     * Prints the tree as an indented structure,
     * with the root indented by the given amount.
     */
    private void print(Tree<V> node, String indent) {
        if (node == null) {
            return;
        }
        System.out.println(indent + node.value);
        for (Iterator<Tree<V>> iter =
                node.children.iterator();
            iter.hasNext();) {
            print(iter.next(), indent + "  ");
        }
    }

    /**
     * Returns a string that, if printed, will show
     * the given node as an indented tree structure.
     */
```

```java
public String toMultilineString() {
    return toMultilineString(this, "");
}

/**
 * Returns a string that, if printed, will show the
 * given node as an indented tree structure, with
 * the initial line prefixed by the indent string.
 */
private String toMultilineString(Tree<V> node,
String indent) {
    if (node == null) {
        return "";
    }
    String result = indent + node.value + "\n";
    if ("block".equals(node.value .toString())) {
        indent += "|";
    }
    for (Iterator<Tree<V>> iter =
            node.children.iterator();
        iter.hasNext();) {
        Tree<V> next = iter.next();
        result += toMultilineString(next,
        indent + "  ");
    }
    return result;
}

/**
 * Parses a string of the general form
 * value(child, child, … , child) and returns the
 * corresponding tree. Children may be separated
 * by commas and/or spaces.
 * Node values are all Strings.
 */
public static Tree<String> parse(String s)
        throws IllegalArgumentException {
    StringTokenizer tokenizer =
```

```java
            new StringTokenizer(s, " (),", true);
    List<String> tokens = new LinkedList<String>();
    while (tokenizer.hasMoreTokens()) {
        String token = tokenizer.nextToken();
        if (token.trim().length() == 0) continue;
        if (token.equals(",")) continue;
        tokens.add(token);
    }
    Tree<String> result = parse(tokens);
    if (tokens.size() > 0) {
        throw new IllegalArgumentException(
            "Leftover tokens: " + tokens);
    }
    return result;
}

/**
 * Parses and returns one tree, consisting of
 * a value and possible children (enclosed in
 * parentheses), starting at the first element
 * of tokens. Returns null if this token is a
 * close parenthesis, or if there are no
 * more tokens.
 */
private static Tree<String> parse(List<String>
tokens)
        throws IllegalArgumentException {
    // No tokens -- return null
    if (tokens.size() == 0) {
        return null;
    }
    // Get the next token and remove it from the list
    String token = tokens.remove(0);
    // If the token is an open parenthesis
    if (token.equals("(")) {
        throw new IllegalArgumentException(
            "Unexpected open parenthesis before " +
            tokens);
    }
```

```
    // If the token is a close parenthesis, we are
    // at the end of a list of children
    if (token.equals(")")) {
        return null;
    }
    // Make a tree with this token as its value
    Tree<String> tree = new Tree<String>(token);
    // Check for children
    if (tokens.size() > 0 &&
        tokens.get(0).equals("(")) {
        tokens.remove(0);
        Tree<String> child;
        while ((child = parse(tokens)) != null) {
            tree.addChild(child);
        }
    }
    return tree;
}


/**
 * Tests whether this tree contains the node
 * passed in as a parameter.
 */
public boolean contains(Tree<V> node) {
    if (this == node)
        return true;
    for (Tree<V> child : children) {
        if (child.contains(node))
            return true;
    }
    return false;
}
}
```

Index

Printed in the United States
by Baker & Taylor Publisher Services